PRAYING

WITH

POWER

DR. STUART PATTICO

Sunesis Publications

COMMENDATIONS FOR 'PRAYING WITH POWER'

Pastor Noel McLean (Senior Pastor of YCF International):

"Dr Pattico, has once again demonstrated his ability to be inclusive in his writing style without removing the depth and gravity of the subject matter.

'Praying with Power', is not merely a timely reminder of the importance of prayer, but a necessary 'call' to revisit what scripture actually teaches about prayer!

With insightful exegesis and clearly defined steps, the reader cannot but help themselves from reaching the place, of 'Praying with Power!' "

Bishop Lenford Rowe (Regional Overseer, Church of God of Prophecy):

"This instructive, informative and qualitative book on prayer is a **must** for anyone who wants to understand the potency, potential and possibilities of prayer. Dr Pattico has captured within these pages, teachings and principles of prayer, that will inform, transform and empower the believer's life. I highly recommend this book."

About the Author

DR. STUART PATTICO is an ordained full-time minister of the gospel. He has an itinerant preaching and teaching ministry, which includes healing meetings, gospel crusades, revivals, prophetic meetings, and conferences. He has ministered in the UK and Overseas.

Dr. Pattico is the author of the books **Praying with Power**, **The Anointing** and **End Times: Are You Prepared?** and has also written booklets on prophetic ministry and dream interpretation. He has also written a study guide called **Understanding the Bible**, and earned his Doctorate in Ministry from Christian Leadership University.

Dr. Pattico is the founder and president of Sunesis Bible College, which is a distance learning online Bible School. He is also the director of Sunesis Publications, which helps Christian authors to publish their books.

Dr. Stuart Pattico is happily married to Minister Andrea Pattico, who is an anointed speaker and worship leader.

For more information and online resources, please visit

WWW.STUARTPATTICO.COM

Acknowledgements

Thanks to my beautiful wife, Minister Andrea Pattico, for your continued love and support.

Thanks also to my mother, Mrs Lilly Liddicott, who helped to proofread this manuscript.

Thanks to all the partners of this ministry.

Thanks to all of you who pray for me and for this ministry.

Thanks, praise, and glory to God the Father, and to His Son Jesus Christ, for all They have done and continue to do.
Amen.

Contents

Ministry Information

Introduction

My goal in writing this book is simple: I want you to receive the answers to your prayers. For this reason, this book explains biblical principles that will help you get those answers. The role of faith, the importance of praying with the whole heart, the power of using Jesus' name, the prayer of command, and hindrances to effective prayer are all covered. The authority you can use in prayer, what you are to pray for, the power of praying in tongues, and how to pray according to the will of God are also dealt with. This book also clears up misunderstandings about prayer by highlighting the differences between prayer in the old and new covenants.

My desire is also that your prayer life will lead you to greater intimacy with the Lord. The last two chapters in this book, which focus on worship, will help you to experience God in fresh ways as you worship Him in spirit and in truth.

I pray that the principles you are about to read will propel you to new heights as you pray with power!

Dr. Stuart Pattico

Chapter 1

What is Prayer?

A simple definition of prayer can be found in the following verse:

> Genesis 26:25 So he [Isaac] built an altar there **and called on the name of the LORD**...

Prayer is simply calling upon God. There are various reasons why we may call upon God. Here are some biblical reasons:

We pray as a way of **drawing nearer to God**:

> Psalm 145:18 The LORD *is* near to all who call upon Him, To all who call upon Him in truth.

Prayer is an excellent way to develop a closer relationship with God.

We may also pray simply **to praise God:**

> Isaiah 12:4 And in that day you will say: "Praise the LORD, call upon His name...

In our prayers, we have an excellent opportunity to express how great God is – this is called praise.

We may also pray **to give God thanks:**

> Psalm 105:1 Oh, give thanks to the LORD! Call upon His name...

Prayer gives us the chance to communicate how grateful we are for all that God has done.

In prayer, we also can **confess our sins.** John the apostle said:

> 1 John 1:9 If we confess our sins, He is faithful and just to forgive us *our* sins and to cleanse us from all unrighteousness.

It is wonderful to know that when we confess our sins to God, He forgives us. He doesn't hold it against us anymore; we are forgiven the moment we confess it to God.

We can also pray in order **to ask God a question**. Through the prophet Jeremiah, God said:

> Jeremiah 33:3 'Call to Me, and I will answer you, and show you great and mighty things, which you do not know.'

It is wonderful to know that we serve a God who is able to speak back to us. He is the living God, and as such, He is able to communicate with us.

Furthermore, we can pray **to make requests of God,** whether for others or ourselves. Jesus said:

> John 16:24 Until now you have asked nothing in My name. Ask, and you will receive, that your joy may be full.

Not only can we ask for things in prayer, we can also expect to receive them! Why? So that "your joy may be full". What a wonderful God we serve! He wants us to be full of joy, and one of the ways this is achieved is through answered prayer.

So, we have seen six reasons why we might pray. In the next chapter, we will look at the importance of praying with faith.

Reflective Questions:

1. How many of these six reasons to pray have been present in your own prayer life?

2. How will you ensure that your prayer life includes all these aspects?

Chapter 2

Praying with Faith

The Bible gives us specific instruction on how we should pray. In this chapter, we will look at the role of faith in prayer.

Jesus taught that when we pray, we should do so in faith:

> Matthew 21:22 And whatever things you ask in prayer, believing, you will receive.

Notice that Jesus conditioned answered prayer on the supplicant "believing". If you believe, then you will receive. But if you doubt, then you'll have to do without! James said:

> James 1:6 But let him ask in faith, with no doubting, for he who doubts is like a wave of the sea driven and tossed by the wind.
> James 1:7 For let not that man suppose that he will receive anything from the Lord;

Notice that the man who doubts should not expect to receive anything from God.

Faith means that we **fully expect** God to actually answer our prayer. We have no doubt whatsoever that He will answer us.

An excellent example of such faith is the woman with the issue of blood, who is described in the following passage:

> Matthew 9:20 And suddenly, a woman who had a flow of blood for twelve years came from behind and touched the hem of His garment.
> Matthew 9:21 For she said to herself, "If only I may touch His garment, **I shall be made well**."
> Matthew 9:22 But Jesus turned around, and when He saw her He said, "Be of good cheer, daughter; **your faith has made you well**." And the woman was made well from that hour.

Notice, the woman did not say "maybe I'll be made well" or "if it is God's will I'll be made well". She said "I **shall** be made well". She *knew that she knew that she knew* that she would be made well. She had no doubt whatsoever. Now, Jesus didn't turn around and accuse her of being presumptuous. No, he called it "faith", and she was made well from that hour.

Someone who prays with faith believes that what he or she is saying is actually happening right there and then. In Mark 11:23, Jesus said the following:

> Mark 11:23 For assuredly, I say to you, whoever says to this mountain, 'Be removed and be cast into the sea,' and does not doubt in his heart, but believes that those things he says will be done, he will have whatever he says.

16

The above translation is not very accurate, as in the original Greek, the phrase "will be done" is in what is called, the *indicative present*. This means that "will be done" should really be translated "is happening". Therefore, the One New Man Bible gives a much more accurate translation of this verse:

> Truly I say to you that whoever would say to this mountain, 'You must immediately be removed and you must immediately be cast into the sea,' and would not doubt in his heart but would **believe that what he is saying is happening**, it will be to him.
> (Mark 11:23, The One New Man Bible)

A person who prays in faith believes that what they are saying is happening as they are saying it. They don't wait until they see it happen before they believe it has happened. They believe that it is happening **when they say it**. Don't wait until you see the answer to your prayers with your physical eyes. Believe that what you are praying for is happening when you are praying it. That's how faith works.

Someone who prays with faith believes that at the moment they prayed, they received the answer. In the next verse, Jesus said:

> Mark 11:24 Therefore I say to you, whatever things you ask when you pray, believe that you receive *them,* and you will have *them.*

The person who prays in faith doesn't believe that they received when they see it with their physical eyes; they believe that they received it when they prayed.

Reflective Questions:

Before you move on to the next chapter, please do the following two things:

1. Think about something you have been praying for. Next, ask yourself this question: do you believe that you have already received it, even if you cannot yet see it with your physical eyes?

2. Think about the way you pray. When you pray, do you consciously believe that what you are saying is happening right there and then?

It is important that we believe that we have received the moment we pray. That is how we pray in faith. We must be convinced that what we are praying for is happening right there and then.

Chapter 3

Praying with Your Whole Heart

In addition to praying with faith, there are other guidelines that the Bible gives us about prayer, one of which is that prayer must be with the whole heart. Prayer must not be mere lip service; it must come from the heart. The Scriptures state:

> Psalm 119:145 I cry out with *my* **whole heart**; Hear me, O LORD! ...

An excellent example of this is Hannah. She was married to Elkanah, who also had another wife called Peninnah. Unlike Peninnah, Hannah was barren and had no children. The Bible tells us that Peninnah tormented and humiliated Hannah year by year because of her barrenness. However, Hannah went to the Lord in prayer. Because she spoke in her heart, but moved her lips, Eli the priest thought she was drunk. In the following verse, we read Hannah's reply to Eli:

> 1 Samuel 1:15 But Hannah answered and said, "...I... have **poured out my soul** before the LORD.

Notice that Hannah "poured out" her soul before God. Now that's praying with the whole heart! This was no casual prayer. This was heartfelt and earnest prayer. The Lord answered her prayer, and she conceived and gave birth to Samuel.

It is very important that we pray with our whole heart. In fact, God is not pleased when we pray half-heartedly. God said:

> Mark 7:6 ...THIS PEOPLE HONORS ME WITH THEIR LIPS, BUT THEIR HEART IS FAR FROM ME.

It is possible to honour God with your lips, yet have your heart far from Him. However, that is not how God wants us to pray. He wants us to pray with our whole heart.

Sometimes, praying with the whole heart will mean that we have to persist in prayer about something. Let us consider the following scenario that Jesus told:

> Luke 11:5 And He [Jesus] said to them, "Which of you shall have a friend, and go to him at midnight and say to him, 'Friend, lend me three loaves;
> Luke 11:6 for a friend of mine has come to me on his journey, and I have nothing to set before him';
> Luke 11:7 and he will answer from within and say, 'Do not trouble me; the door is now shut, and my children are with me in bed; I cannot rise and give to you'?
> Luke 11:8 I say to you, though he will not rise and give to him because he is his friend, yet **because of his persistence** he will rise and give him as many as he needs.
> Luke 11:9 "So I say to you, [you must continually] ask, and it will be given to you; [you must continually] seek,

and you will find; [you must continually] knock, and it will be opened to you.

In verses 5 – 8, Jesus tells us about a man who went to his friend at midnight to ask him for three loaves of bread. As the friend was in bed, he was not willing to get up and give him the bread. However, because of the man's persistence, the friend got up and gave him the bread. Jesus then applies this scenario to our prayer life by stating that if we "ask", "seek", and "knock", we too will get what we want. In the original language, the three verbs "ask", "seek", and "knock" are all in what is called the *imperative present*. This means that continuous action is being spoken of. Jesus is telling us to continually ask, continually seek and continually knock. We are to persist in prayer.

Several chapters later, Jesus gives us another lesson on praying with persistence:

> Luke 18:1 Then He spoke a parable to them, that men always ought to pray and not lose heart,
> Luke 18:2 saying: "There was in a certain city a judge who did not fear God nor regard man.
> Luke 18:3 Now there was a widow in that city; and she came to him, saying, 'Get justice for me from my adversary.'
> Luke 18:4 And **he would not for a while**; but afterward he said within himself, 'Though I do not fear God nor regard man,

Luke 18:5 yet because this widow troubles me I will avenge her, lest by **her continual coming** she weary me.' "

Luke 18:6 Then the Lord said, "Hear what the unjust judge said.

Luke 18:7 And shall God not avenge His own elect who cry out day and night to Him, though He bears long with them?

Luke 18:8 I tell you that He will avenge them speedily. Nevertheless, when the Son of Man comes, will He really find **faith** on the earth?"

In this parable, a widow wanted justice from an unjust judge. At first, the judge wouldn't give her what she wanted, but because she kept coming, he gave in, lest she should wear him out. Jesus used this parable to teach us that we "always ought to pray and not lose heart". However, as we keep coming to God in prayer about something, it is imperative that we do so in faith. We are not to keeping coming to God in unbelief. We must believe that what we are praying is happening. Indeed, Jesus' final challenge in verse 8 is "will He really find **faith**?" when He comes. For example, when we are praying for our nation, we need to keep on praying. No matter how bad things are looking, we must not give up. We must keep on praying, but we must do so in faith. We must believe that God is answering our prayers.

Chapter 4

Praying to the Father

The Bible reveals that there is one God, and that within the one Godhead, there are three persons – the Father, the Son, and the Holy Spirit. Jesus taught us that the person we are to direct our prayers to is the Father. He said:

> John 16:23 "And in that day you will **ask Me nothing**. Most assuredly, I say to you, whatever you **ask the Father** in My name He will give you.

There are Christians who begin their prayers, "Dear Jesus...". However, this is not what Jesus taught. He taught us to prayer to the Father. However, I don't wish to be legalistic about this, as there are biblical examples of people praying to Jesus after His ascension, and so we can still speak to Jesus in our prayers (e.g. Acts 7:54-60). Indeed, I once was in a predicament in which I literally found myself unable to breathe. I cried out "JESUS!!!" and immediately I was delivered and breath came to me again. Hallelujah!

However, it is clear that Jesus is telling us to direct our requests to the Father, and so prayer requests are to normally be directed to God the Father. As Jesus said,

> Luke 11:2 ..."When you pray, say: **Our Father** in heaven

It is important that we not only call God "Father", but we also relate to Him as our Father. Doing so will take remove a lot of pressure from us, because a father is responsible for looking after his children. When you know that God is your Heavenly Father, you will worry a lot less.

Also, knowing that God is your Father will mean that you are not afraid to approach Him. God doesn't want us to be afraid of Him. Paul the apostle wrote this:

> Romans 8:15 For you did not receive the spirit of bondage again to fear, but you received the Spirit of adoption by whom we cry out, "Abba, Father."

Notice that the Holy Spirit does not cause us to "fear". God doesn't want us to be afraid of Him. Instead, the Holy Spirit is the "Spirit of adoption", who enables us to cry out "Abba, Father". "Abba" is an Aramaic word that means "father". According to the Gemara, which is a Rabbinical commentary on the Mishna (the traditional teaching of the Jews), slaves were forbidden to use "Abba" when addressing the head of the family. Whether or not that was the case, it is clear from Romans 8:15 that God is not a cruel slave-master. He has adopted us into His family and we can call Him "Abba"! Hallelujah! God wants a close, intimate relationship with us. The Holy Spirit enables us to have a love-relationship with God in which we are not afraid of Him, but instead relate to Him as "Daddy".

However, not everyone has had a positive experience of his or her earthly father. If you are not careful, you can project the image of your earthly father onto your Heavenly Father. For example, some earthly fathers were not there at all in their children's life, which may cause the children to have difficulty in seeing their Heavenly Father as always being there for them. Also, if a child did not have a close, joyful relationship with his earthly father, that child may initially not envision God as wanting to have an intimate and joyful relationship with him. However, Jesus informs us that God wants to have an intimate relationship with us. He said:

> John 17:3 And this is eternal life, that they may know You, the only true God, and Jesus Christ whom You have sent.

Eternal life is knowing God. The Greek word translated "know" in this verse can speak of intimacy, and that is exactly what our Heavenly Father wants – a close, intimate relationship with His children.

Our Heavenly Father is not like many of our earthly fathers. And even if you had an excellent, kind, and loving earthly father, our Heavenly Father is still greater! This is because our Heavenly Father is Perfect Love. John the apostle wrote this about Him:

> 1 John 4:16 ... God is love...

Our Father in heaven is so very loving, and He Himself is love. In fact, if we wish to know what our Heavenly Father is like, all we need to do is look at Jesus. Our Lord Jesus perfectly reveals the Father, insomuch that He said:

> John 14:9 ... He who has seen Me has seen the Father...

To see the Father, you simply need to look at Jesus. The saying "like father, like son" certainly applies to the Godhead! As you think about Jesus, know that your Heavenly Father is just like Him!

Reflective Questions:

In closing, please carefully think through the following questions, so that you can ensure you have the correct view of God:

1. If you know / knew your earthly father, what is / was he like?

2. How has this influenced the way you see your Heavenly Father?

3. Now think about Jesus. In what way does He change the way you envisage your Heavenly Father?

Chapter 5

Praying in the Name of Jesus

In the last chapter, we saw that we are to address our prayers to the Father. However, Christ also taught that when we pray to the Father, we are to do so in Jesus' name:

> John 14:13 And whatever you **ask in My name**, that I will do, that the Father may be glorified in the Son.
> John 14:14 If you **ask anything in My name**, I will do *it*.

> John 15:16 You did not choose Me, but I chose you and appointed you that you should go and bear fruit, and *that* your fruit should remain, that whatever you **ask the Father in My name** He may give you.

> John 16:23 "And in that day you will ask Me nothing. Most assuredly, I say to you, whatever you **ask the Father in My name** He will give you.

I have heard several people end their prayers "in the name of the Father, Son, and Holy Spirit". However, Jesus never told us to pray that way. We are only commanded to baptise in the name of the Father, Son and Holy Spirit. When it comes to prayer, we are to pray in the name of Jesus.

This is very important, and is distinctive to the New Covenant era. In the Old Testament, they didn't pray in the name of Jesus. However, in the New Testament, there is a new way to pray, and that is in the name of Jesus.

So, what is the significance of the name of Jesus? Paul the apostle wrote the following about Jesus:

> Philippians 2:9 Therefore God also has highly exalted Him and given Him **the name which is above every name**,

The name of Jesus is above every other name. This means that the name of Jesus is the most authoritative name in the universe. That's the name that we pray in, and so when we pray in the name of Jesus, we are praying with authority.

But why is Jesus' name above every other name? Well, when Adam sinned, the devil got power over mankind, insomuch that Paul the apostle refers to the devil as "the god of this age" in the following verse:

> 2 Corinthians 4:4 whose minds the **god of this age** has blinded, who do not believe, lest the light of the gospel of the glory of Christ, who is the image of God, should shine on them.

Paul also calls the devil "the prince of the power of the air":

Ephesians 2:2 ...**the prince of the power of the air**, the spirit who now works in the sons of disobedience,

The devil gained these titles when Adam sinned. The devil gained control over the world, insomuch that the apostle John says the following:

1 John 5:19 ... and **the whole world lies *under the sway of* the wicked one**.

Furthermore, when Adam sinned, the devil gained something called "the power of death":

Hebrews 2:14 ...that through death He might destroy **him who had the power of death**, that is, the devil,

When Adam sinned, the devil obtained the power of death and he became the god of this age. That's why the world is in such a mess. That's why there is all this sickness, poverty, and sin. It's because the devil is the god of this age. That's why the Bible says that Jesus healed all "who were oppressed of the devil" (Acts 10:38). The devil is behind the mess that we see. But thanks be to God, Jesus Christ came, and became the sacrifice for our sins on the cross. Hallelujah!

Now, before Jesus came, the Israelites were commanded to observe the Day of Atonement each year, in which atonement was made for the people. There were **two goats.** One was sacrificed and the other goat was called the scapegoat. The scapegoat, would carry away the peoples' sins to the wilderness. As the Bible states:

> Leviticus 16:21 Aaron shall lay both his hands on the head of the live goat, confess over it all the iniquities of the children of Israel, and all their transgressions, concerning all their sins, putting them on the head of the goat, and shall send *it* away into the wilderness by the hand of a suitable man.
>
> Leviticus 16:22 The goat shall bear on itself all their iniquities to an uninhabited land; and he shall release the goat in the wilderness.

Even so, after He died on the cross as the sacrifice for our sins, Jesus carried away our sins far away into the realm called Hades so that "as far as the east is from the west, so far has He removed our transgressions from us" (Psalm 103:12). This is borne witness to in the following verses:

> Ephesians 4:9 (Now this, "HE ASCENDED"—what does it mean but that **He also first descended into the lower parts of the earth**?

> Acts 2:31 he... spoke concerning the resurrection of the Christ, that **His soul was not left in Hades**, nor did His flesh see corruption

Notice that according to Ephesians 4:9, before Jesus ascended to heaven, He first descended into the lower parts of the earth. Peter the apostle calls this region "Hades" in Acts 2:31. According to Peter, Jesus was resurrected so that "His soul was not left in Hades".

Now, there are those who mistakenly believe that Jesus went to a place called "Paradise" when He died. This is due to a mistranslation of Luke 23:43. For more information about this, please see the Appendix at the back of this book.

So, we have seen from Acts 2:31 that Jesus' soul went to a place called Hades when He died. The particular compartment of Hades that Jesus went to is called the Abyss. Paul the apostle makes this plain in the following verses:

> Romans 10:6 But the righteousness of faith speaks in this way, "DO NOT SAY IN YOUR HEART, 'WHO WILL ASCEND INTO HEAVEN?' " (that is, to bring Christ down *from above*)
> Romans 10:7 or, " 'WHO WILL DESCEND INTO **THE ABYSS**?' " (that is, to bring Christ up from the dead).

In these verses, Paul identifies heaven as the place where Christ presently is ("'Who will ascend into heaven?' that is, to bring Christ down from above"), and the Abyss as the place where Christ was when He was dead ("'Who will descend into the abyss?' that is, to bring Christ up from the dead").

So what exactly is the Abyss? It is a place of torment that even the demons are afraid of. This is made clear when we compare the following two parallel passages, both of which describe Jesus' encounter with a man who had a legion of demons:

> Luke 8:30 Jesus asked him, saying, "What is your name?" And he said, "Legion," because many demons had entered him.
> Luke 8:31 And they begged Him that He would not command them to go out into the **abyss**.

> Matthew 8:29 And suddenly they cried out, saying, "What have we to do with You, Jesus, You Son of God? Have You come here to **torment** us before the time?"

We see from these passages that the demons associated the abyss with "torment".

From the following verse, we learn that the Abyss is ruled by an angelic being called Destruction

> Revelation 9:11 And they [the tormenting locusts] had as king over them the angel of the bottomless pit [Greek = the abyss], whose name in Hebrew *is* Abaddon [Destruction]...

The Greek word translated "bottomless pit" is the same word translated "abyss" elsewhere. Acts 2:24 indicates that Jesus was in agony when He was there:

> [24]But God raised Him [Jesus] up again, putting an end to **the agony** of death, since it was impossible for Him to be held in its power.
> (Acts 2:24 NASB)

When Jesus was resurrected, it put an end to "the agony of death" that He was enduring. But why was Jesus in "agony"? Well, when Jesus got to the Abyss in Hades, the demons must have been excited, thinking that they had finally got the Son of God. I believe they were so excited that they invited the devil himself to come and see. They then afflicted Jesus greatly. This affliction is depicted in the following psalm, which ultimately is a prophetic psalm about Jesus (i.e. a *messianic psalm*):

> Psalm 88:6 You have laid me in the lowest pit, In darkness, in the depths.
> Psalm 88:7 Your wrath lies heavy upon me, And You have afflicted me with all Your waves. Selah
> Psalm 88:8 You have put away my acquaintances far from me; You have made me an abomination to them; **I am shut up, and I cannot get out.**..
> Psalm 88:16 Your fierce wrath has gone over me; Your terrors have cut me off.

Psalm 88:17 They came around me all day long like water; They engulfed me altogether.

We see from the above description, that Jesus suffered a great ordeal whilst He was dead and in the Abyss in Hades. But then, in the midst of His affliction, something amazing happened - the power of the Holy Spirit came upon Jesus, and he threw all the demons off him, and disarmed and defeated every one of them, and publicly humiliated them. Paul the apostle describes this in Colossians 2:15:

Colossians 2:15 Having **disarmed** principalities and powers, He [Jesus] made a public spectacle of them, triumphing over them in it.

Hallelujah! When Jesus was in Hades, He disarmed the principalities and powers. The Revised Version translates it a little differently, shedding further light on what happened:

Colossians 2:15 having **put off from himself** the principalities and the powers, he made a show of them openly, triumphing over them in it.
(Revised Version)

The phrase "put off from himself" indicates that Jesus threw off from Himself all the demons that had jumped on him to afflict Him. When the devil saw Jesus disarming and throwing them off Him, he must have been alarmed and overcome with fear at the sight of Jesus throwing them aside with great power. Indeed, the devil started to shake in his

34

boots!   And then, after Jesus dealt with all those principalities and powers, He turned to the devil, and said, "Now, I'm coming for you!". What happened next is described in Hebrews 2:14:

> Hebrews 2:14   ... through death He [Jesus] ...**destroy[ed] him** who had the **power of death**, that is, **the devil**,

Through death, Jesus **destroyed** the devil. In the original language, "destroy" means to render inoperative and inactive. It means to deprive of force, influence and power. It means to paralyse!   In other words, Jesus gave the devil such a severe beating that he was left paralysed, and the effects of that beating last to this day.   And then, having thrown off the demons and having destroyed the devil, Jesus rose up victorious from the grave!

Notice that according to Hebrews 2:14, the devil had the "power of death". After Jesus defeated with the devil, He took something away from him. He took away the power of death from devil. Yes, Jesus took away the devil's power! Let us notice what the resurrected Jesus said to John the apostle:

> Revelation 1:18 I *am* He who lives, and was dead, and behold, I am alive forevermore. Amen. And **I have the keys of Hades and of Death**.

Jesus said that He has the keys of Hades and of Death. The devil no longer has the power of death; Jesus has taken it from him. In other words, Jesus was saying, "I've taken away the devil's power, and now I have all authority". When Jesus dealt the devil that knockout blow, He took away the keys from the devil. Previously, the devil had "the power of death" (Hebrews 2:14). But now, it has been taken away from him. Now Jesus has all authority. Therefore, after His resurrection, Jesus said to His disciples:

> Matthew 28:18 ...**All authority** has been given to Me in heaven and on earth.

Jesus has "all authority" now, in heaven **and** on earth. Jesus doesn't just have all authority in heaven, He has all authority on earth too. Also, notice that Jesus didn't say "Some authority is given to Me". No, He said "**all** authority has been give to Me...". Well, if Jesus has **all** authority, it means something very simple – it means the devil has none! Jesus has taken it from him. The devil has absolutely no authority now. Jesus now sits in the heavenly places, having taken away all of the devil's authority. Jesus now has all authority, and His name is far above every other name. Consider what Paul the apostle said about our exalted Saviour:

> Ephesians 1:20 ... [God] raised Him [Jesus] from the dead and seated *Him* at His right hand in the heavenly *places,*
> Ephesians 1:21 **far above** all principality and power and might and dominion, and every name that is

named, not only in this age but also in that which is to come.

Jesus Christ, the name above all other names, is seated "far above" all of the devil's forces. Notice, it is not just "above", it is "**far** above". There isn't even a contest. The devil doesn't even come close. Jesus defeated Him totally and is the Lord of all.

But someone might ask: if Christ has taken away the devil's power, why is the world still as it is? Why is there still sickness, disease and sin if the devil has been defeated? Well, the answer is found in the following passage written by Paul the apostle:

> "and He made all things subject under His [Jesus'] feet and gave Him authority over everyone in the congregation [church], which is **His body, the extension** of the One Who fills everything in every way."
>
> (Ephesians 1:22-23, The One New Man Bible)

Christ has gone back to heaven. However, this verse informs us that we are the "extension" of Christ to earth. In other words, it is we, the body of Christ, who are to administer His authority on the earth. He has given us His authority to execute on earth – we are His extension on the earth. It is through us, that Christ's authority is to be extended to the earth. Consider how Paul the apostle described us in the following passage:

37

> Ephesians 2:5 [God] made us alive together with
> Christ (by grace you have been saved),
> Ephesians 2:6 and raised *us* up together, and made
> *us* sit together in the heavenly *places* in Christ Jesus

When Jesus was resurrected, having thrown off the principalities and powers that were afflicting him and having defeated the devil, we were raised up with Him. God "made us alive together with Christ". We now partake of Christ's authority, insomuch that we are presently seated in Him in the heavenly places.

Notice that we are seated in Christ in the heavenly places. Now, where are these heavenly places where Christ is seated? Let's look at Ephesians 1:20-21 again:

> Ephesians 1:20 ... [God] raised Him [Jesus] from
> the dead and seated *Him* at His right hand in the
> heavenly *places,*
> Ephesians 1:21 **far above all principality and
> power** and might and dominion, and every name that
> is named, not only in this age but also in that which is
> to come.

Christ Jesus is seated "far above all principality and power", and you are sitting there with Him! Hallelujah! When you pray, you are not to pray as though you are a victim of the devil. No, you are seated in Christ Jesus far above the devil. The devil's authority has been taken away, and you now

38

have authority over him. Jesus has given His authority to you, and you are to use it! Consider what Christ has said to us:

> Luke 10:19 Behold, I give you the authority to trample on serpents and scorpions, and over all the power of the enemy, and nothing shall by any means hurt you.

We have authority over **all** the power of the enemy. The devil has nowhere to hide; we have authority over **all** his power. Jesus has given us His authority to execute on the earth.

We must understand that we have Jesus' authority here and now. Peter the apostle knew what He had, and on a certain occasion, he and the apostle John came across a lame man who was begging. Let's see how Peter responded:

> Acts 3:6 Then Peter said, "Silver and gold I do not have, but **what I do have** I give you: In **the name** of Jesus Christ of Nazareth, rise up and walk."

Notice that Peter said, "but what I do **have** I give you". Notice that Peter knew what He had. I trust that you also know that you have the authority of Christ too! And so, when Peter exercised that authority by saying "**in the name of Jesus Christ,** rise up and walk", he was using the authority that Jesus has given to all of us.

Let us pay particular attention to the fact that Peter exercised this authority by using the name of Jesus. It was by the name of Jesus Christ that this man was healed. Peter later said the following about this miracle:

> Acts 4:10 let it be known to you all, and to all the people of Israel, that **by the name of Jesus Christ** of Nazareth, whom you crucified, whom God raised from the dead, by Him this man stands here before you whole.

This is precisely why we are to pray in the name of Jesus. When we pray in Jesus' name, we are exercising Christ's authority on the earth. When we pray in the name of Jesus Christ, we are exercising the authority of Jesus! And when you pray in that authority, the devil is already defeated. When we pray in the name of Jesus, we are enforcing the total victory that Jesus won over all the demons, and the total destruction that He dealt to the devil when He was in Hades, taking away his keys and rising from there completely victorious. We have been raised with Him, and we have total authority in His name. When we use the name of Jesus, we enforce the fact that devil's keys have been taken away by Jesus! Hallelujah!

When you use the name of Jesus, make sure that you use it in faith. It's important that you believe in its authority and power. Its important that you use it knowing that Jesus destroyed the devil and his demons in Hades and rose from grave having taken away the devil's power. We must use the name of Jesus in faith. In the miracle we have just read about, faith was present. Peter said about this healing:

> Acts 3:16 And His [Jesus'] name, **through faith in His name**, has made this man strong...

It was faith in the name of Jesus that made the man strong. So next time you pray; be sure to pray in faith, and to pray in the name of Jesus!

Reflective Questions:

1. How will knowing what Jesus accomplished in Hades give you greater confidence when you use the name of Jesus?

2. To what extent are you aware of the great authority you have through Christ?

Chapter 6

The Power of Praying in Tongues

It is important that our study of prayer is informed by the New Testament, and not only the Old Testament. This is because there is a radical difference between prayer under the New Covenant and Old Covenant eras. Now that Jesus has shed His blood and risen from the grave, we are under the New Covenant (Matthew 26:28; Hebrews 8:6). We have already seen that in the New Covenant, we pray in the name of Jesus. Another difference is that in the New Covenant, there are two ways to pray.

Let us consider something that Paul said about prayer:

> 1 Corinthians 14:15 What is *the conclusion* then? I will pray with the spirit, and I will also pray with the understanding. I will sing with the spirit, and I will also sing with the understanding.

In this verse Paul identifies two ways to pray:

1. With the spirit
2. With the understanding

But what does it means to pray with the spirit? Paul answers this question in the previous verse:

43

1 Corinthians 14:14 For if I pray in a **tongue**, **my spirit prays**, but my understanding is unfruitful.

To pray with your spirit is to pray in a tongue, whereas to pray with your understanding is to pray in one's native language (e.g. English).

To pray in a tongue means to pray in a language that is given supernaturally by the Holy Spirit. This is made clear in Acts 2:4 which states:

> Acts 2:4 And they were all filled with the Holy Spirit and began to speak with other tongues, as **the Spirit gave them utterance**.

Tongues are languages that are unknown to the speaker, but are spoken as the Holy Spirit gives the utterance. In the following verse, Paul the apostle informs us that these languages can be either human or angelic:

> 1 Corinthians 13:1 Though I speak with the tongues of men and of angels....

There are two ways that the gift of tongues is used. When the Bible mentions speaking in tongues, we must know which of the two is being referred to, as the two are not the same. The two ways are as follows:

1. Speaking in tongues to communicate a message from God to the church:

Regarding this use of tongues, Paul wrote the following:

> 1 Corinthians 14:21 In the law it is written: "WITH MEN OF OTHER TONGUES AND OTHER LIPS I **WILL SPEAK** TO THIS PEOPLE...

Notice that God says "I will speak to this people". In this use of tongues **God is speaking to man**. It is not man speaking to God, it is God speaking to man. In order for the message to be understood, the gift of interpretation is needed. Therefore, about this use of tongues, Paul wrote:

> 1 Corinthians 14:27 If anyone speaks in a tongue, *let there be* two or at the most three, *each* in turn, and **let one interpret**.

Not everyone will be used to speak in tongues in this way i.e. to speak a message from God to people in tongues. This is what Paul meant when he asked the following question:

> 1 Corinthians 12:30 ...Do all speak with tongues?...

His question anticipates a negative answer. But he is referring to tongues that communicate a message from God to the church. Not everyone will be used in that way. However, there is another use of tongues that is available to every believer...

2. Praying to God in tongues

Regarding this use of tongues, Paul wrote the following:

> 1 Corinthians 14:14 For if I pray in a **tongue**, **my spirit prays**, but my understanding is unfruitful.

Notice that in this use of tongues, it is not God speaking to man. Rather, in this use of tongues, **man is speaking to God**. This is evident from the fact that Paul described his spirit as praying in this use of tongues. Furthermore, Paul stated the following about this use of tongues:

> 1 Corinthians 14:2 For he who speaks in a tongue **does not speak to men** but to God…

Let us pay careful attention to this difference. About this use of tongues, Paul states that the speaker is not speaking to men, but is speaking to God. This is because in this use of tongues, the speaker is praying. Therefore, this type of tongues is also known as your **prayer language**.

Unlike the previous use of tongues where God speaks to man, everyone can expect to receive their prayer language. It is available to everyone. Speaking about praying in tongues, Paul said:

> 1 Corinthians 14:5 Now I want you **all** to speak in tongues… (ESV)

46

Notice that Paul wanted "all" the believers to use their prayer language. This use of tongues is available to all believers and is the kind of tongues that Jesus said would be accessible to every Christian:

> Mark 16:17 And these signs will follow those who believe: In My name they will cast out demons; **they will speak with new tongues**;

So, if you are a believer, then this wonderful gift is available to you.

But what is the point of praying in tongues, and in what way does it benefit you? We will now look at five things that happen when you pray in tongues.

1. Your spirit prays

When you pray in tongues, it is not your mind praying, it is your spirit. Paul wrote:

> 1 Corinthians 14:14 For if I pray in a **tongue, my spirit prays**, but my understanding is unfruitful.

Because your understanding (i.e. your mind) is not involved, you become more sensitive to your spirit when you pray in tongues. This is a very important benefit, but in order to appreciate this, we must first understand the following about the human spirit.

Your spirit is your innermost being. In the following passage, the human spirit is called "the hidden man of the heart":

> 1 Peter 3:4   But *let it be* the **hidden man of the heart**, in that which is not corruptible, *even the ornament* of a meek and quiet **spirit**...
> (KJV)

Notice that our spirits are "not corruptible". The Bible reveals that we are spirit, soul, and body (1 Thessalonians 5:23). Our soul, which is the seat of our natural emotions, may experience different moods. Our body may feel hungry. If we are not careful, both of these can affect the quality of our prayers. Indeed, Isaac asked for food before he blessed his son (Genesis 27:7)! But our spirit is incorruptible. Our spirits are not subject to hunger or mood swings.

Our spirits are incorruptible because they are the part of us that has become "born again". Jesus said:

> John 3:6   That which is born of the flesh is flesh; and that which is born of the Spirit is spirit.

The part of us that is born of the Holy Spirit is our spirit. Our born-again spirit is the "new creation" that Paul mentions in 2 Corinthians 5:17. It is the "new man" that has been recreated in the image of God.

> Ephesians 4:24 ...put on the new man which was created according to God, in true righteousness and holiness.

> Colossians 3:10 [you] have put on the new *man* who is renewed in knowledge according to the image of Him who created him

Our spirit is already perfect and fully saved. Our souls and our bodies haven't reached there yet, but our spirit is already fully saved and fully perfected. Therefore a key to living the victorious Christian life is to become more spirit-conscious, and make decisions based on our spirit, instead of based on our souls and bodies. When we live only according to our souls, we are what the Bible calls "sensual" (James 3:15). "Sensual" is a translation of the Greek word *psuchikos*, which is from the word *psuche*, which means "soul". When we live only according to the body, we are what the Bible calls "carnal" (*sarkikos*) which is from the Greek word for "flesh" (*sarx*) (1 Corinthians 3:3; Romans 8:1). However, we are to be spiritual people (1 Corinthians 3:1), and when we pray in tongues, we grow in sensitivity to our spirits, because it is our incorruptible spirit that is praying.

Your human spirit is also the part of you that knows everything about you. Paul wrote:

> 1 Corinthians 2:11 For what man knows the things of a man except the spirit of the man which is in him?

49

Therefore, by praying in tongues, you are able to pray about anything that concerns you perfectly – your spirit has complete knowledge about you!

Your spirit is also the part of your being that the Holy Spirit speaks from. Jesus said:

> **38** He who believes in Me, as the Scripture said, '**From his innermost being** [i.e. his spirit] will flow rivers of living water.'" **39 But this He spoke of the Spirit**, whom those who believed in Him were to receive
> (John 7:38-39 NASB)

In this verse, Jesus likened the Holy Spirit to rivers of living water which will flow from our innermost being (i.e. our spirit). Notice that the Holy Spirit flows from our spirits. That is the place where God's voice is heard from when He speaks to us. Again, Paul the apostle wrote:

> Galatians 4:6 And because you are sons, God has sent forth the Spirit of His Son into your hearts, crying out, "Abba, Father!"

The Holy Spirit has come into our hearts. We saw earlier that our spirit is the hidden man of our heart. When the Holy Spirit came to live in our hearts, He joined Himself to our spirits. That's why Paul the apostle also said:

> 1 Corinthians 6:17 But he who is joined to the Lord is one spirit *with Him.*

The Holy Spirit is one with your spirit. Therefore, when the Holy Spirit speaks to you, He will speak to you from your spirit, because that is where He is. When we pray in tongues, we increase our sensitivity to our spirits, which is the place where the Holy Spirit speaks to us from. We therefore increase our sensitivity to the voice of God when we pray in tongues.

2. You access the hidden wisdom of God

When we pray in tongues, we access the hidden wisdom of God. In the following verse, the apostle Paul states that when someone speaks in a tongue, they are speaking "mysteries":

> 1 Corinthians 14:2 For he who speaks in a tongue does not speak to men but to God, for no one understands *him;* however, in the spirit **he speaks mysteries**.

What are these mysteries? Well, let us consider something that Paul said elsewhere in his letter to the Corinthians:

> 1 Corinthians 2:7 But we speak **the wisdom of God in a mystery**, the **hidden *wisdom*** which God ordained before the ages for our glory

51

Paul claimed to speak the hidden wisdom of God in a mystery, and when we pray in tongues, we are speaking forth those mysteries; we are speaking forth the hidden wisdom of God! Praying in tongues was a tool that Paul used to access this wisdom, and this is made evident in the following passage:

> 1 Corinthians 14:18 I thank my God I speak with tongues more than you all;
> 1 Corinthians 14:19 yet in the church I would rather speak five words with my understanding, that I may teach others **also...**

In verse 18, when Paul thanked God that he spoke in tongues more than all the Corinthians, he is referring to praying in tongues in a private setting. We know this is so because in the next verse he says "yet in the church I would rather speak five words with my understanding...". However, Paul doesn't stop there. He says that the reason he wants to speak with his understanding in church is so that he "may teach others **also**". In other words, when he was praying in tongues in private, he was teaching himself. And when he got to church, he wanted to teach others "also". The word "also" means "in addition to". So he wanted others to be taught in addition to himself, because he received teaching when he prayed in tongues in private. No wonder he thanked God that he spoke in tongues more than all of them – he was being taught the wisdom of God as he did so. Hallelujah! And you can receive the same as you spend time praying in tongues. Through praying in tongues, you access the hidden wisdom of God!

But why is this so? How is it that through praying in tongues we access God's wisdom? Well, David said:

> Psalm 51:6 Behold, You desire truth in the inward parts, And **in the hidden** *part* **You will make me to know wisdom**.

Notice where God makes us to know wisdom. It is in "the hidden part", which is a reference to the human spirit. God makes us to know wisdom in our spirits. When we pray in tongues, our spirit is praying. Our spirit is activated, and the wisdom of God in our spirit flows to us.

3. You offer up perfect praise to God

Another wonderful benefit of praying in tongues is that it enables you to offer perfect praise to God. The logic of this is really quite simple. When we speak in tongues, it is the Spirit of God who gives us the utterance:

> Acts 2:4 And they were all filled with the Holy Spirit and began to speak with other tongues, as the Spirit gave them utterance.

Therefore, when we are praising God in tongues, we are speaking words given by the Holy Spirit. Now, the Holy

Spirit knows exactly how God wishes to be praised because He knows God perfectly. This is made plain by the apostle Paul in the following verse:

> 1 Corinthians 2:11 For what man knows the things of a man except the spirit of the man which is in him? Even so no one knows the things of God except the Spirit of God.

Because the Holy Spirit knows God perfectly, when He gives us a language with which we can praise God, it is perfect praise. That tongues can be used to praise and thank God is evident from the following passage written by Paul:

> 1 Corinthians 14:15 What is *the conclusion* then? I will pray with the spirit, and I will also pray with the understanding. I will sing with the spirit, and I will also sing with the understanding.
> 1 Corinthians 14:16 Otherwise, if you bless with the spirit, how will he who occupies the place of the uninformed say "Amen" at your giving of thanks, since he does not understand what you say?
> 1 Corinthians 14:17 For **you indeed give thanks well**, but the other is not edified.

Notice that Paul refers to singing with the spirit (i.e. singing in tongues). We can sing songs of praise to God in tongues. However, in a public church service, if you were asked to pray, and you only prayed in tongues, those of us who are in tune with the Spirit would be able to say "Amen", but "he who occupies the place of the uninformed" won't understand what is going on. Therefore, he will not be able to say "Amen". For this reason, Paul says that he will pray with the understanding also in a public church service. But I would like to draw your attention to what Paul says in verse 17. He says that when you pray in tongues, "you indeed give thanks well". In the original Greek, the word "well" is *kalōs* which means "beautifully", "finely", and "excellently". When you give God thanks in tongues, your thanksgiving is beautiful, fine and excellent! Hallelujah!

Have you ever wanted to praise God, but can't quite find the words to adequately express how you feel? Well, God has given you a language that you can use to praise Him! On the Day of Pentecost, when 120 disciples were baptised in the Holy Spirit, they began to speak in other tongues as the Spirit gave them utterance. There were people who heard them and who also understood the languages they were speaking, and this is what they reported:

> Acts 2:11 [the people then said] we hear them speaking in our own tongues **the wonderful works of God.**"

How great it is to declare the wonderful works of God, and when you praise Him in other tongues, that's exactly what you are doing.

4. You pray according to the perfect will of God

Let us look again at Acts 2:4:

> Acts 2:4 And they were all filled with the Holy Spirit and began to speak with other tongues, as **the Spirit gave them utterance**.

We see from this verse that tongues are spoken as the Spirit gives utterance. Your tongues come from the Holy Spirit, and therefore whatever you pray in tongues is the perfect will of God. Consider what Paul the apostle wrote in the following verse:

> Romans 8:27 Now He who searches the hearts knows what the mind of the Spirit *is,* because **He [the Spirit] makes intercession for the saints according to *the will of* God**.

According to the above verse, whatever the Holy Spirit prays is according to the will of God.

Through praying in tongues for yourself, you can bring your life into alignment with the perfect will of God.

Through praying in tongues for others, you can bring their lives into alignment with the perfect will of God.

Through praying in tongues regarding situations, you can bring situations into alignment with the perfect will of God.

If the church got together (e.g. in a believers' prayer meeting), and prays in tongues for the church, the church can be brought into alignment with the perfect will of God.

Why can all this happen? Because when you pray in tongues, you are praying the perfect will of God! This is a wonderful benefit of praying in tongues.

5. You are building yourself up in God

Paul wrote the following about praying in tongues:

> 1 Corinthians 14:4   He who speaks in a tongue edifies himself...

When you pray in tongues, you are edifying yourself. The Greek word translated "edifies" means to build a house. When you pray in tongues, you are building yourself stronger and more powerful in God. Consequently, you become a spiritual force to be reckoned with! No wonder the apostle Paul was such a powerful man of God, he prayed in tongues more than all the Corinthians put together!

> 1 Corinthians 14:18 I thank my God I speak with tongues more than you all;

So, those are five benefits to praying in tongues. In the next chapter, we will look at three things we can do to begin using our prayer language.

Reflective Questions:

1. How do you think the above five benefits of praying in tongues can impact your life?

2. Do you think you could spend more time praying in tongues in order to experience these benefits more in your life?

Chapter 7

How to Use Your Prayer Language

In this chapter, we will briefly look at three simple keys that will help you to begin using your prayer language. They are as follows:

1. Get rid of wrong beliefs about tongues

Sometimes, people are hindered from using their prayer language because of faulty beliefs about tongues. For example, some people think that not everyone can receive the gift of praying in tongues, and that it is only for a certain people. However, this is not true. Paul the apostle wrote:

> 1 Corinthians 14:5 Now I want you **all** to speak in tongues... (ESV)

God wants every believer to speak in tongues. We have seen in the last chapter how powerful praying in tongues is, and God wants all His children to benefit from it. But someone might say, "Didn't Paul say 'Do all speak with tongues?' in 1 Corinthians 12:30?" Yes, he did say that, but as we saw in the last chapter, he was taking about speaking a message in tongues to the church; he wasn't talking about tongues as a prayer language. God wants all His children to receive their prayer language.

2. Ensure you have received your prayer language (tongue)

Some people find that they can only speak in tongues when they feel especially inspired by the Holy Spirit to do so.

However, when you are activated in your prayer language, you will be able to pray in tongues whenever you want to, just like when you pray in English. If this were not the case, Paul would not have needed to write to the Corinthians to give them instructions on how to use tongues in church (1 Corinthians 14:23-28). It was precisely because they could speak in tongues as they willed that he had to give them guidelines on how to use it.

When you receive your prayer language, you will be able to build up yourself whenever you want to by praying in tongues. Because I have received my prayer language, I can start speaking in tongues whenever I wish to, and I can stop whenever I wish to.

If you have not yet been activated in your prayer language, here are some steps that you can follow in order to freely receive this wonderful gift:

I. Get into the presence of God

You can enter God's presence by praising Him:

> Psalm 100:4 Enter into His gates with thanksgiving, *And* into His courts with praise. Be thankful to Him, *and* bless His name.

As you enter into His presence with praise, you are ready for the next step.

II. Ask God to fill you with His Spirit and to give you your prayer language

Jesus said:

> John 16:24 … Ask, and you will receive, that your joy may be full.

If you've already been filled with the Holy Spirit, that's fine, just ask God to fill you anyway. The Bible teaches that we are to be continuously filled with the Spirit (Ephesians 5:18). If you haven't yet been filled with the Holy Spirit, get ready, because you are about to be!

So, simply ask God to fill you with His Spirit and to give you your prayer language. And then move on to the next step.

III. Believe that you have received

Jesus said:

Mark 11:24 ... whatever things you ask **when you pray, believe that you receive** *them,* and you will have *them.*

This is very important. Once you have asked God to fill you with His Spirit, you must believe that He has done so; you must accept and believe that it is done. Verbalise your faith by saying, "I believe I have received, thank You Lord for filling me with Your Spirit and for giving me the gift of praying in other tongues". Then you can move on to the next step:

IV. Stop speaking in English

You are about to speak in other tongues, but you can't speak in two languages at the same time! Therefore, stop speaking in your native language, and get ready to speak in other tongues. It is very important that you do not speak another word in your native language.

V. Begin to speak in other tongues

The Holy Spirit will not force you to speak in tongues. Notice that in Acts 2:4, the Bible doesn't say that the Holy Spirit spoke in tongues, it says that "they" (i.e. those who were filled) spoke in tongues:

Acts 2:4   And **they**... began to speak with other tongues, as the Spirit gave them utterance.

When Jesus came walking on water to the disciples, He didn't force Peter to get out of the boat and start walking on the water.

> Matthew 14:26   And when the disciples saw Him walking on the sea, they were troubled, saying, "It is a ghost!" And they cried out for fear.
> Matthew 14:27   But immediately Jesus spoke to them, saying, "Be of good cheer! It is I; do not be afraid."
> Matthew 14:28   And Peter answered Him and said, "Lord, if it is You, command me to come to You on the water."
> Matthew 14:29   So He said, "Come." And when Peter had come down out of the boat, he walked on the water to go to Jesus.

Peter had to make a decision to get out of the boat, and then to walk on water.   Peter had to leave what he knew (the boat) and step out into the unknown (the water).   Peter didn't know He could walk on water until He tried, and you won't know you can speak in tongues until you try.   So, you need to stop speaking in English (get out of the boat, leave the known) and start speaking the syllables that flow forth from your spirit (walk on water, you don't know you can until you put your foot on the water and try!).   **You won't necessarily hear new words in your mind**.   You just need to start speaking in faith the syllables that will flow forth from your spirit, and God will form them into your new prayer language. Just trust Him, He will do it!

If you have not yet received your prayer language, then I encourage you to take the time right now to follow those five steps, and to allow God to give you this blessing. Amen.

We will now look at the third key that will help you to begin using your prayer language.

3. Once you have received your prayer language, begin to use it each day in your personal time of prayer

Paul the apostle said this to the Corinthians:

> 1 Corinthians 14:18 I thank my God I speak with tongues more than you all

Paul thanked God that He spoke in tongues more than all of them. Evidently, Paul spent a lot of time praying in tongues, and I would recommend that you aim to do the same. You may start with five minutes a day. By an act of the will, you can decide that you will spend the next five minutes praying in tongues. Remember, your mind will not necessarily get anything out of it, because it is your incorruptible spirit that is doing the praying:

1 Corinthians 14:14 For if I pray in a tongue, my spirit prays, but my understanding is unfruitful.

But as you pray in tongues, something wonderful is happening, you are building yourself up strong in the Lord:

1 Corinthians 14:4 He who speaks in a tongue edifies [builds up] himself...

Also, as it is your spirit praying, you are growing in sensitivity to your spirit. As you get comfortable praying in tongues for around five minutes, seek to increase the amount of time. For example, you can increase it 10 minutes, and then you can go on to increase it to 15 minutes, and then to 25 minutes, and 30 minutes etc. As you do this, you are entering into a glorious realm of prayer, and your spiritual life will be forever transformed!

Reflective Question:

1. How will you begin to include more praying in tongues in your times of prayer? Ask the Lord to lead you in this.

Chapter 8

What to Pray For – Part 1

So far, we have seen that prayer is calling upon God. We have seen that we are to pray in faith (believing that what we are saying is happening when we say it) and that we are to pray with our whole heart. We have also seen that we are to pray to the Father in the name of Jesus, and that praying in tongues is a powerful way to pray. In the next few chapters we will now look at seven things that the Church is commanded to pray for in the New Testament.

Pray for the purposes of God

When teaching on prayer, Jesus said the following:

> Matthew 6:9   In this manner, therefore, pray: Our Father in heaven, Hallowed be Your name.
> Matthew 6:10   Your kingdom come. Your will be done On earth as *it is* in heaven.

It is important to realize that in the original Greek, the words "Hallowed", "come", and "done" are all in what is called the *imperative mood*. In other words, they are all firm requests. In this prayer, "Hallowed be Your name", "Your kingdom come", and "Your will be done" are three **requests** that are being made. When Jesus taught us to pray "Hallowed be Your name", His point was not that we should begin prayer with worship (as important as worship is). "Hallowed be Your name" is actually a firm request, which is clear from the mood in the original Greek. To "hallow" means to make holy or to venerate. Jesus is teaching us that our first priority in prayer is God's name. We are to pray that God's name be regarded as holy by all people. Wouldn't you love it if in your nation, when God or Jesus were mentioned, that people would have a great reverence for His name? Don't you want the name of God to be honoured throughout your land? Well, that is to be our first priority in prayer – the honour of God's name. We don't want God's name to be taken lightly, disrespected, or used as a swear word. We want God's name to be honoured by all people, and that is our number one priority in prayer.

Elijah is an excellent example of someone who prioritized the honour of God's name in prayer. By God's instruction, Elijah had challenged the prophets of Baal to see if their god would answer by fire. Nothing happened when those prophets prayed. But let us consider the prayer that Elijah made when it was his turn:

> 1 Kings 18:37 Hear me, O LORD, hear me, that this people may know that You *are* the LORD God, and *that* You have turned their hearts back *to You* again."
> 1 Kings 18:38 Then the fire of the LORD fell and consumed the burnt sacrifice, and the wood and the stones and the dust, and it licked up the water that *was* in the trench.

Notice what Elijah's motive was in his prayer: "that this people may know that You *are* the LORD God". Elijah's primary concern was that God be glorified, and that needs to be our chief goal too.

Hezekiah is another example of someone whose prayer was motivated by the glory of God's name. When the nation was threatened by the king of Assyria, this is how Hezekiah prayed:

> 2 Kings 19:19 Now therefore, O LORD our God, I pray, save us from his hand, that all the kingdoms of the earth may know that You *are* the LORD God, You alone."

Again, let us notice what Hezekiah's motive was: "that all the kingdoms of the earth may know that You *are* the LORD God, You alone". The glory of God's name needs to be our main priority in prayer. The following two verses from Psalm 66 are a good illustration of what it will look like when God's name is hallowed:

> Psalm 66:3 Say to God, "How awesome are Your works! Through the greatness of Your power Your enemies shall submit themselves to You.
> Psalm 66:4 All the earth shall worship You And sing praises to You; They shall sing praises *to* Your name." Selah

This is a beautiful description, which ties in very closely with the next request in the prayer that Jesus taught us – "Your

69

kingdom come". The kingdom of God is the reign of God. Notice that in the above passage, God's enemies are described as submitting themselves to Him. Jesus said this about the kingdom of God:

> Matthew 12:28 But if I cast out demons by the Spirit of God, surely the kingdom of God has come upon you.

When the demon enemies of God start submitting themselves, it is a sign that the kingdom of God has arrived. We are to pray, "Your kingdom come". We want the reign of God to be established and the works of the devil to be dismantled! That's why Jesus told His disciples to heal the sick. Sickness is a work of the devil (Acts 10:38). Our business is to dismantle the devil's works and to release the reign of God. That's why Jesus connected healing the sick with the kingdom of God. He said to His disciples:

> Luke 10:9 And heal the sick there, and say to them, 'The kingdom of God has come near to you.'

When we heal the sick, it means that the kingdom of God has come to those who are healed. This is the reign of God. It is the influence of the Holy Spirit, in whom we walk in righteousness, peace and joy (Romans 14:17). The Spirit of God destroys the works of Satan, and releases the glories of God's reign.

Then, Jesus told us to pray "Your will be done, on earth as it is in heaven". A lot of Christians have completely misunderstood the will of God. If something bad happens, or if a loved one dies, they may say, "Oh, it was the will of God that such and such happened". But this is a complete misunderstanding of what Jesus said here. The fact that Jesus told us to pray that God's will be done on earth indicates that presently, **God's will is not being done on earth**. If God's will were being done on earth, there would be absolutely no point in us praying, "Your will be done, on earth as it is in heaven". The fact that Jesus instructs us to pray this shows us that God's will is not being done on earth. For example, there are people who are starving right now. That certainly is not God's will. Yet it is happening. There are many people who have died early since you have been reading this book. That certainly isn't God's will. In fact, several of those people may well have gone to hell when they died. We know from the Scriptures that this not God's will:

> 2 Peter 3:9 The Lord is not slack concerning *His* promise, as some count slackness, but is longsuffering toward us, **not willing that any should perish** but that all should come to repentance.

The fact is, many things happen on earth today that are not God's will. Therefore, if something bad happens, don't be so quick to say "it was the will of God". That's not fair on God, as there are many things happening today that are not God's will.

71

How then can we know what God's will is? Well, Jesus told us in the very same sentence:

> Matthew 6:10 Your kingdom come. Your will be done On earth **as *it is* in heaven**.

Notice that Jesus told us to pray that God's will be done "on earth **as it is in heaven**". In heaven, God's perfect will is being done right now. If you want to know what the will of God is, just look at heaven! In heaven you won't find people sinning, getting sick, starving or living in poverty. Why? Because these things are not God's will. Therefore, if someone is sick, you are to pray for their healing. Why? Because in heaven there is no sickness, and we are to pray that God's will be done on earth, as it is in heaven. We have a part to play in God's will being done here on earth as it is in heaven. God is waiting for us to use the authority He has given us to release the kingdom of God. That's why Jesus said the following to Peter:

> Matthew 16:19 And I will give you the keys of the kingdom of heaven, and whatever you bind on earth will be bound in heaven, and whatever you loose on earth will be loosed in heaven."

This kingdom power was not only for Peter, because Jesus said to the other disciples that they had the same authority two chapters later:

72

> Matthew 18:18 "Assuredly, I say to you, whatever you bind on earth will be bound in heaven, and whatever you loose on earth will be loosed in heaven.

The original context of this saying of Jesus is in His teaching regarding dealing with a brother who sins against you. However, this saying is not limited to that context. This is evident from the use of the word "whatever". We can bind (i.e. tie up) or loose (i.e. release, set free) "whatever". In other words, nothing is excluded; our authority to release the reign of God extends to "whatever"! Hallelujah! But notice how this authority is again connected with heaven. In the translation used above, it says that whatever we bind or loose on earth "will be bound/loosed in heaven". In the original Greek, the verbs in the phrases "bound in heaven" and "loosed in heaven" are in what is called the *participle perfect*. This means that "will be bound" can be more accurately translated "having been bound"; and "will be loosed" can be more accurately translated "having been loosed". Therefore, the LITV more accurately translates the verse as follows:

> Matthew 18:18 Truly I say to you, Whatever you bind on the earth will be, having been bound in Heaven. And whatever you loose on the earth will be, having been loosed in Heaven. (LITV – Green's Literal Translation)

In other words, as we release God's kingdom reign on earth, we are synchronising earth with heaven. We are bringing situations on earth into perfect agreement with the perfect will of God as manifested in heaven. Through prayer, we become co-labourers with God, becoming vessels through which God's will is done on earth, even as it is in heaven.

It is vitally important that in prayer, we see ourselves as "kings". Now that Jesus has taken away the devil's keys of authority, prayer is no longer about begging God to do this or that. For starters, we are His children and have bold access to Him through the blood of Jesus. This is made clear in the following verse:

> Hebrews 10:19   Therefore, brethren, having **boldness** to enter the Holiest by the blood of Jesus,

We are to approach God with confidence! We are not to approach Him as beggars. Even if you see examples in the Bible, where people approach God as though they are beggars, please note that such examples took place before Jesus died on the cross for our sins. We now have a new covenant, which is superior to the old one, as stated in Hebrews 8:6:

> Hebrews 8:6   But now He has obtained a more excellent ministry, inasmuch as He is also Mediator of a better covenant, which was **established on better promises**.

74

But to some, this may seem to be somewhat arrogant. After all, how can we humans approach the Almighty in this way? The answer is quite simple – we are His children! And Daddy loves it when His children come to Him. The blood of Jesus has washed away our sins. And even if we commit a sin, we can confess it to Him and He instantly forgives us:

> 1 John 1:9 If we confess our sins, He is faithful and just to forgive us *our* sins and to cleanse us from all unrighteousness.

Furthermore, as we have been raised up together with Christ, we share in His royalty. He is King, we also are kings. Consider how Peter described us:

> 1 Peter 2:9 But you *are* a chosen generation, a **royal** priesthood...

We are not just a priesthood, we a royal priesthood. We are royalty; we partake of Christ's kingship. The New Testament refers to us as "**joint heirs** with Christ" (Romans 8:17). In Revelation 5:10, we are explicitly referred to as "kings":

> Revelation 5:9 ... You were slain, And have redeemed us to God by Your blood Out of every tribe and tongue and people and nation,
> Revelation 5:10 And have made us **kings** and priests to our God; And we shall reign on the earth."

Well, what is the responsibility of a king? A king has authority, and with that authority he is to reign! In Romans 5:17, Paul says the following about us:

> Romans 5:17 ...those who receive abundance of grace and of the gift of righteousness will **reign** in life through ... Jesus Christ.

If you have put your faith in Jesus Christ, then you have received abundance of grace and the free gift of righteousness. This means that you will reign in life! In this verse, The Amplified Bible translates "will reign" as "will reign as kings". As kings we are to reign, and that is your portion. In prayer, we are to use the authority that Jesus has given us to see to it that God's name is hallowed, that His kingdom comes, and that His will is done on earth, as it is in heaven.

Pray for secular leaders

Paul wrote the following to Timothy:

> 1 Timothy 2:1 Therefore I exhort first of all that supplications, prayers, intercessions, *and* giving of thanks be made for all men,
> 1 Timothy 2:2 for kings and all who are in authority, that we may lead a quiet and peaceable life in all godliness and reverence.
> 1 Timothy 2:3 For this *is* good and acceptable in the sight of God our Savior,

1 Timothy 2:4 who desires all men to be saved and to come to the knowledge of the truth.

It is so important that we pray for "kings and all who are in authority". We are to pray for the leaders of our nations. But why should we pray for them? God has only instructed us to pray for them because He fully intends on answering our prayers! Jesus said:

John 16:24 ... Ask, and **you will receive**, that your joy may be full.

Therefore, when we pray for our leaders, let us pray with faith - believing that what we are saying is happening.

How should we pray for our nations' leaders? Well, we can pray that they would rule with wisdom. The Bible says:

Proverbs 8:12 "I, wisdom, dwell with prudence...
Proverbs 8:15 By me [wisdom] kings reign, And rulers decree justice.

The leaders of our nations have very difficult decisions to make. Let us pray that God would pour out the Spirit of wisdom on them.

We can also pray that they would rule and conduct their duties in righteousness. The following passage indicates that God wants kings who reign in righteousness:

Isaiah 32:1   Behold, a king will reign in righteousness, And princes will rule with justice.

Justice and righteousness are very important to God, and there are numerous scriptures that speak about this.

As we pray for our leaders, we must also remember that God is able to direct their hearts. The Bible states:

Proverbs 21:1 The king's heart *is* in the hand of the LORD, *Like* the rivers of water; He turns it wherever He wishes.

Therefore, if leaders are making plans and proposing laws that are contrary to righteousness, we can pray that God would change their heart.

However, if we are going to pray for our leaders, it is essential that we have the proper attitude towards them. Consider what Peter the apostle said about how we should be towards secular leaders:

1 Peter 2:13   Therefore submit yourselves to every ordinance of man for the Lord's sake, whether to the king as supreme,

1 Peter 2:14 or to governors, as to those who are sent by him for the punishment of evildoers and *for the* praise of those who do good.

> 1 Peter 2:15   For this is the will of God, that by doing good you may put to silence the ignorance of foolish men—
>
> ...
>
> 1 Peter 2:17   Honor all *people.* Love the brotherhood. Fear God. Honor the king.

We are to submit to them, and we are to honour them. Of course, if they ask us to do something that is contrary to what the Bible teaches, we are not to obey such orders. In such cases, like the apostles, we can say, "we ought to obey God rather than men" (Acts 5:29). However, as a general rule, we are to be submissive to our secular leaders. Let us read what the apostle Paul said about the rulers and police officers of his day:

> Romans 13:1   Let every soul be subject to the governing authorities. For there is no authority except from God, and the authorities that exist are appointed by God.
>
> Romans 13:2   Therefore whoever resists the authority resists the ordinance of God, and those who resist will bring judgment on themselves.
>
> Romans 13:3   For rulers are not a terror to good works, but to evil. Do you want to be unafraid of the authority? Do what is good, and you will have praise from the same.
>
> Romans 13:4   For he is God's minister to you for good. But if you do evil, be afraid; for he does not

bear the sword in vain; for he is God's minister, an avenger to execute wrath on him who practices evil.

Romans 13:5 Therefore you must be subject, not only because of wrath but also for conscience' sake.

Romans 13:6 For because of this you also pay taxes, for they are God's ministers attending continually to this very thing.

Romans 13:7 Render therefore to all their due: taxes to whom taxes are due, customs to whom customs, fear to whom fear, honor to whom honor.

Paul states that the authorities have been "appointed by God". The logical outcome of this is that if we resist those authorities, we are resisting God Himself. Furthermore, the rulers and police are "God's minister", able to execute wrath on those who practice evil. In light of all this, as Christians, we should be diligent in paying our taxes and in showing them honour.

It is actually to our advantage that we pray for our secular leaders. Paul wanted Christians to pray for secular leaders "that we may lead a quiet and peaceable life in all godliness and reverence" (1 Timothy 2:2). This thought is echoed in Jeremiah 29:7 which was written to God's people who were carried away captive to Babylon:

Jeremiah 29:7 ... seek the peace of the city where I have caused you to be carried away captive, and pray to the LORD for it; for in its peace you will have peace.

Paul the apostle prayed that Israel would be saved. He said:

> Romans 10:1 Brethren, my heart's desire and prayer to God for Israel is that they may be saved.

We too can pray that God would save our nation. As we pray for our nation and its leaders, there will be peace. And in that peace, we also will have peace.

Reflective Questions:

1. According to the Bible, what is heaven like? How does this affect your understanding of God's will?

2. Do you believe you may have underestimated the extent to which we have authority on earth?

3. What is your attitude towards secular authorities, such as the government and the police? Do you think you need to adjust the way you view and speak about them?

Chapter 9

What to Pray For – Part 2

Pray that God would send out workers

In the following passage, Jesus also taught that we should pray to God that He would send out workers:

> Matthew 9:36 But when He saw the multitudes, He was moved with compassion for them, because they were weary and scattered, like sheep having no shepherd.
>
> Matthew 9:37 Then He said to His disciples, "The harvest truly *is* plentiful, but the laborers *are* few.
>
> Matthew 9:38 Therefore pray the Lord of the harvest to send out laborers into His harvest."

I wonder why Jesus told us to pray this. Wouldn't God take it upon Himself to send out preachers of the gospel with or without our prayers? Why should He need us to pray that He would? This shows us how important prayer is: clearly, God wants us to join with Him in the great work that is to be done, and one of the ways we do this is through prayer. If we want to see the nations transformed, then we must pray that God would send out workers to reach those who need to be reached. The good news is that when we pray along these lines, God will answer us. Workers will be sent out, people will be saved and delivered, and God will be glorified.

Pray for existing preachers of the gospel

Not only are we to pray that God would send out workers, we are also to pray for those He has already sent. Paul the apostle wrote the following to the Ephesian believers:

> Ephesians 6:18 praying always with all prayer and supplication in the Spirit, being watchful to this end with all perseverance and supplication for all the saints—
>
> Ephesians 6:19 **and for me**, that utterance may be given to me, that I may open my mouth boldly to make known the mystery of the gospel,

Notice that in verse 19, Paul specifically requested that they pray for him, particularly for boldness to make known the mystery of the gospel. We need to do the same for preachers today. Preachers must never yield to intimidation, but must preach the word with boldness. They need prayer. The devil hates the gospel, and we can be sure that he particularly targets those who have devoted themselves to preaching it. In the following passage, Paul asked the Colossian believers to pray for him and his team:

> Colossians 4:2 Continue earnestly in prayer, being vigilant in it with thanksgiving;
>
> Colossians 4:3 meanwhile praying also for us, that God would open to us a door for the word, to

84

> speak the mystery of Christ, for which I am also in chains,
>
> Colossians 4:4 that I may make it manifest, as I ought to speak.

This time, Paul wanted the believers to pray that God would open to them a door for the word. We need to pray that God would open doors for those He has sent. Paul also wanted prayer so that he would make the mystery of Christ "manifest". In other words, Paul wanted the gospel to be shown in all its glory. When the gospel is preached in all its glory to every nation, only then will the end come. Jesus said:

> Matthew 24:14 And this gospel of the kingdom will be preached in all the world as a witness to all the nations, and then the end will come.

Notice that Jesus said that the gospel is to be preached as a "witness". We can be sure that the witness that Jesus speaks of is a true, total, and complete testimony. We don't need just any gospel to be preached. We need **the** gospel to be preached, and it needs to be preached in all its fullness. It needs to be made "manifest". We need to pray that preachers will preach the gospel of Jesus Christ in such a way that it is shown in all it glory.

An important part of preaching the gospel is the demonstration of its power. Paul the apostle said the following:

85

Romans 15:18 For I will not dare to speak of any of those things which Christ has not accomplished through me, in word and deed, to make the Gentiles obedient—

Romans 15:19 in mighty signs and wonders, by the power of the Spirit of God, so that from Jerusalem and round about to Illyricum I have fully preached the gospel of Christ.

Paul stated that the words, deeds, mighty signs and wonders Christ accomplished though him in the Spirit's power, were so that he "fully preached the gospel of Christ". When we pray for preachers of the gospel, we need to pray that God would confirm the word with such signs and wonders following. In Acts 4, the apostles Peter and John were arrested and commanded not to speak to anyone in the name of Jesus. In response to this threat, the believers prayed, and here is part of what they said:

Acts 4:29 Now, Lord, look on their threats, and grant to Your servants that with all boldness they may speak Your word,

Acts 4:30 by stretching out Your hand to heal, and that signs and wonders may be done through the name of Your holy Servant Jesus.

First they prayed that they would speak the word with all boldness. This is what Paul asked the Ephesians to pray for him. But then, they also prayed that God would stretch forth

His hand to heal, and that signs and wonders would be done through the name of Jesus. We need to pray for the same thing today.

When writing to the Romans, Paul requested that the believers pray for his protection (Romans 15:30-31). It is important that we pray for preachers' protection. Interestingly, Paul also requested that they prayed that his service for Jerusalem would be acceptable to the saints (Romans 15:31). This is a reference to the contribution he was carrying for the poor among the saints in Jerusalem (Romans 15:26). For Paul, such deeds were part of fully preaching the gospel of Christ (Romans 15:18-19).

When writing to the Thessalonians, Paul asked them to pray for him, Silvanus, and Timothy, that the word of the Lord would have free course and be glorified, just as it had with them, and that they would be delivered from "unreasonable and wicked men" (2 Thessalonians 3:1-2). This again highlights the themes of protection, and the importance of the word going forth and having the glorious effect that God wants it to have.

Reflective Questions:

1. Why is it so important that you pray for those who minister God's word?

2. How will this impact your prayer life?

Chapter 10

What to Pray For – Part 3

Pray for all the saints

It is important that we pray for all the saints. The New Testament uses the word "saints" to refer to all believers. Paul said the following to the Ephesians:

> Ephesians 6:18 praying always with all prayer and supplication in the Spirit, being watchful to this end with all perseverance and supplication **for all the saints—**

Notice that Paul says that we are to pray for the saints "in the Spirit". It is so important that in all our prayers we are led by the Holy Spirit. We must learn to sense the direction that the Spirit would have us to pray, and that direction will be sensed in our spirits. As discussed earlier, an excellent way to develop sensitivity to our spirits is through praying in tongues.

We also see examples in the Bible of how we are to pray for the saints. In John 17, Jesus prayed that believers would be kept from the evil one (John 17:11,15), that they would have His joy fulfilled in them (John 17:13), that they would be sanctified by God's truth (John 17:17), that they would be one (John 17:21), and that they would be with Him where He is (John 17:24).

Paul the apostle prayed for the Roman believers that they would be of one mind (Romans 15:5-6). He prayed that the Philippians' love would abound more and more in knowledge and discernment; that they would approve the things that are excellent, and that they would be sincere and without offence till the day of Christ. He also prayed that they would be filled with the fruits of righteousness (Philippians 1:9-11). For the Ephesians, Paul made a very interesting prayer:

> Ephesians 1:15 Therefore I also, after I heard of your faith in the Lord Jesus and your love for all the saints,
> Ephesians 1:16 do not cease to give thanks for you, making mention of you in my prayers:
> Ephesians 1:17 that the God of our Lord Jesus Christ, the Father of glory, may give to you the spirit of wisdom and revelation in the knowledge of Him,
> Ephesians 1:18 the eyes of your understanding being enlightened; that you may know what is the hope of His calling, what are the riches of the glory of His inheritance in the saints,
> Ephesians 1:19 and what is the exceeding greatness of His power toward us who believe, according to the working of His mighty power
> Ephesians 1:20 which He worked in Christ when He raised Him from the dead and seated Him at His right hand in the heavenly places,

90

First of all, Paul was diligent to give thanks for these saints. Giving thanks for the saints is an important part of praying for them. Then, Paul prayed that God would give them a spirit of wisdom and revelation. Why did Paul want them to have wisdom and revelation? So that they would know "the riches of the glory" of God's inheritance "in the saints". Notice that the glory is "in" the saints. Within each of us, there is great glory that God has placed there, and here Paul was praying that these believers would know this glory. But what is this glory? Well, according to verses 19 and 20, this glory is the power that raised Jesus from the dead. The same power that enabled Jesus to throw off and disarm all the principalities, to destroy the devil and to rise up completely victorious.... that same power is in you and me! Hallelujah! Let's look at verses 19 and 20 again:

> Ephesians 1:19 and what is the exceeding greatness of His power toward us who believe, according to the working of His mighty power
> Ephesians 1:20 which He worked in Christ when He raised Him from the dead and seated Him at His right hand in the heavenly places,

Paul is praying that they would know the greatness of this power that is toward us who believe. This is the same power that raised Jesus from the dead. The devil doesn't want us to realise the power that is at work in us. He wants to blindfold us to this reality. The devil realises that once we know the glory that is in us, he is in serious trouble. This is

91

because we will then realise that the devil is truly defeated, and that we share the nature and glory of our Lord Jesus Christ!

God wants to give us the spirit of wisdom and revelation so that we can see this great and awesome power that is at work within us. It is important that as we pray for the saints, we pray that they will know this glory that God has placed in them. This power is infinite in its ability, for Paul writes:

> Ephesians 3:20 Now to Him who is able to do exceedingly abundantly above all that we ask or think, **according to the power that works in us**

God is able to do far beyond anything we can utter or imagine. But the power that can do this is already at work inside of us. May God help us to realise the great power and glory that He has in the saints.

Paul also prayed that the Ephesians would be strengthened with might, that Christ may dwell in their hearts through faith, that they would be rooted and grounded in love, that they would have comprehension of Christ's love, and that they would be filled with all the fullness of God (Ephesians 3:14-19). For the Colossians, Paul prayed that they would be filled with the knowledge of God's will in all wisdom and spiritual understanding. He prayed that they would walk worthy of the Lord, be fruitful in every good work, be increasing in the knowledge of God, and that they would be strengthened with all might for all patience and longsuffering

92

with joy (Colossians 1:9-11). For the Thessalonians, Paul prayed that they would increase and abound in love to one another and to all, and that their hearts would be established blameless in holiness (1 Thessalonians 3:12-13). He prayed that God would sanctify them completely, and that their spirits, souls, and bodies would be preserved blameless at the coming of Jesus Christ (1 Thessalonians 5:23). There are also other prayers that Paul prayed for them in 2 Thessalonians 1:11-12 and 2:16-17, which includes prayer for worthiness of calling, comfort and stability. John the apostle prayed for Gaius, saying:

> 3 John 1:2 Beloved, I pray that you may prosper in all things and be in health, just as your soul prospers.

God wants us to prosper and to be in health. These are all examples of the kinds of prayers we can pray for believers.

Notice that John didn't pray that Gaius would be poor and sick! God wants His children to be prosperous and healthy, and it is important that we pray that way. James wrote the following:

> James 5:13 Is anyone among you suffering? Let him pray. Is anyone cheerful? Let him sing psalms.
> James 5:14 Is anyone among you sick? Let him call for the elders of the church, and let them pray over him, anointing him with oil in the name of the Lord.

> James 5:15 And the prayer of faith will save the sick, and the Lord will raise him up. And if he has committed sins, he will be forgiven.
>
> James 5:16 Confess your trespasses to one another, and **pray for one another, that you may be healed**. The effective, fervent prayer of a righteous man avails much.

Let us note that it is not only elders who can pray for the sick. Verse 16 says "pray for one another, that you may be healed". We can all pray for the sick. Also, let us notice that James does not put suffering and sickness in the same category. Some Christians teach that as believers we are called to suffer and that sickness is part of that suffering. Whilst it is true that we are called to suffer persecution for Christ's sake, persecution is not to be confused with sickness. We may well die as martyrs as a result of persecution, but when it comes to sickness God wants us to be healed. Martyrdom and sickness are two completely different things. This distinction is made very clear in the above passage. When it comes to suffering, James says:

> James 5:13 Is anyone among you suffering? Let him pray....

But when it comes to sickness, James says something entirely different. He says:

James 5:14 Is anyone among you sick? Let him call for the elders of the church, and let them pray over him, anointing him with oil in the name of the Lord.

James 5:15 And **the prayer of faith will save the sick, and the Lord will raise him up**. And if he has committed sins, he will be forgiven.

In this passage, God makes a clear promise that "the prayer of faith will save the sick". The Greek word translated "save" is *sozo* which is also translated "made well" in Matthew 9:21-22 when the woman with issue of blood was healed. The truth is that healing is part of our salvation. Jesus did not only carry our sins when He died, He also took away our sicknesses! This is made clear from the following passage:

Isaiah 53:4 Surely He has borne our griefs And carried our sorrows; Yet we esteemed Him stricken, Smitten by God, and afflicted.

Isaiah 53:5 But He was wounded for our transgressions, He was bruised for our iniquities; The chastisement for our peace was upon Him, And by His stripes we are healed.

In this passage, the prophet Isaiah is speaking about the suffering of Jesus Christ on our behalf. The word "our" is used five times to identify us as the persons for whom Christ suffered this ordeal. In verse 4, Christ is said to have "borne our griefs and carried our sorrows". The Hebrew word translated "griefs" is *choliy*. This word appears 24 times in the Old Testament, and 21 times it is translated "disease",

95

"sick" or "sickness" in the KJV. The Hebrew word translated "sorrows" also means "pain". Therefore, Isaiah is saying that Jesus bore our sicknesses, diseases, and pains. This is made clear when Matthew quotes this verse in his Gospel:

> Matthew 8:16 When evening had come, they brought to Him [Jesus] many who were demon-possessed. And He cast out the spirits with a word, and healed all who were sick,
> Matthew 8:17 that it might be fulfilled which was spoken by Isaiah the prophet, saying: "HE HIMSELF TOOK OUR INFIRMITIES AND BORE OUR SICKNESSES."

Matthew, writing in Greek, uses the words "infirmities" (*astheneia*) and "sicknesses" (*nosos*) when quoting Isaiah 53:4. Furthermore, Matthew is writing in the context of Jesus healing physical sicknesses (v16). Matthew states that Jesus "took" them (v17). This is clear proof that Isaiah is referring to physical healing. But whose sicknesses did Jesus take? The passage states "He Himself took OUR infirmities…". "Our" refers to you and me. It refers to all human beings. Even as Isaiah stated that Jesus was wounded for "our" transgressions, so he states that Jesus bore "our" sicknesses, pains and diseases:

> Isaiah 53:4 Surely He has borne **our** griefs [sicknesses, diseases] And carried **our** sorrows [pain]; Yet we esteemed Him stricken, Smitten by God, and afflicted.

Isaiah 53:5   But He was wounded for **our** transgressions, He was bruised for **our** iniquities; The chastisement for **our** peace was upon Him, And by His stripes we are healed.

Hallelujah! Jesus' healing ministry on earth testified to the fact that He was the Messiah who would take the infirmities and sicknesses of all humanity.   Therefore, Isaiah the prophet states: "by His stripes **we** are healed" (Isaiah 53:5). Because Jesus has taken our sin and sicknesses away, we don't need to carry them anymore. For this reason, James is able to state:

James 5:15 And **the prayer of faith will save the sick, and the Lord will raise him up**. And if he has committed sins, he will be forgiven.

The prayer of faith accesses what Jesus has done for us on the cross. But notice that it is the prayer "of faith". When we pray for the saints, we can't be in two minds about whether or not God wants them well. It is always God's will to heal the sick. This is evident from the fact that Jesus has already taken the sicknesses of the whole world. In fact, to ask if it is God's will to heal is to ask the wrong question. If anything, you should be asking how to receive the healing that God has already provided through Jesus Christ.   Even as we don't need to ask if it is God's will that someone be saved, we don't need to ask if it His will that someone be healed. The sacrifice of Jesus has taken care of both sin and sickness.   That it is always God's will to heal is also

97

evidenced by the fact that Jesus healed everyone who came to Him for healing. Jesus never asked if it were God's will to heal an individual. He just went ahead and healed them and Jesus told His disciples to follow Him (e.g. Matthew 4:19). He never turned anyone away who wanted healing, and Jesus said, "He who has seen Me has seen the Father" (John 14:9). Jesus is the perfect revelation of God. If you want to know God's will for the saints regarding healing, just look at Jesus. Jesus healed them all. Which of you, having children, and if your child were sick and you had the power to instantly heal them, wouldn't you do so? Of course you would, and you would do so simply because you love that child. Well, this is what Jesus said:

> Matthew 7:11 If you then, being evil, know how to give good gifts to your children, how much more will your Father who is in heaven give good things to those who ask Him!

If you would be willing to heal your child, how much more willing is God to heal His children? After all, Jesus suffered, not only to take our sins, but also to take our sicknesses too. This is also why we should make effort to look after our bodies and health. God's wants us well. Therefore, when you pray for the saints, pray with certainty that God wants them well; and pray in faith, believing that what you are saying is happening right there and then.

Now, some may say, "But what about Paul. Didn't he have a thorn in the flesh that God didn't take away?" Well yes, Paul did (2 Corinthians 12:7-9). However, this "thorn in the flesh" was not a sickness. In fact, Paul told us exactly what this "thorn" was. He said it was "a messenger of Satan to buffet me, lest I be exalted above measure" (2 Corinthians 12:7). In other words, it was a demonic angel sent to harass him. Furthermore, the phrase "a thorn in the flesh" was an idiom, similar to our expression "pain in the neck". When we call something or someone a pain in the neck, we don't mean that they are a literal pain in the neck. It is an expression that simply means "something annoying". Even so, "a thorn in the flesh" is an expression that means exactly the same thing. We see this in the Old Testament when Israel's enemies were referred to as "thorns in your sides":

> Numbers 33:55 But if you do not drive out the inhabitants of the land from before you, then it shall be that those whom you let remain shall be irritants in your eyes and **thorns in your sides**, and they shall harass you in the land where you dwell.

Notice that Israel's enemies are referred to as "thorns in your sides". Now, this passage certainly does not mean that Israel's enemies were a sickness or disease! It is simply saying that they would be a nuisance to them. They would "harass" them. When Paul used the expression "thorn in the flesh" he meant exactly the same thing. He was saying that this demonic angel was sent to harass him, most likely through the persecution and opposition to the gospel that he stirred against Paul. Jesus didn't remove this "thorn" from Paul. As noted earlier, we will have to endure persecution

99

for the sake of the gospel. Paul said to Timothy that all who desire to live godly in Christ Jesus will suffer persecution (2 Timothy 3:12). However, this persecution is not to be confused with sickness. They are two separate things.

Again, someone might say "But what about Job? Wasn't it God's will that Job should be sick?" Well, the simple answer to that is this – Job was healed! The book of Job does not end with Job being sick with the sickness the devil put on him; it ends with him being healed, and the latter days of Job were more blessed than his beginning. Let us also remember that Job lived before Jesus came and took away our sins, our sicknesses, and the devil's power. According to some, Job even lived before Abraham. If this were the case, then Job wouldn't have had any covenant of healing. Yet, he was still healed. God wants people to be well. The following Scriptures bear witness to this:

> Exodus 23:25 "So you shall serve the LORD your God, and He will bless your bread and your water. And **I will take sickness away from the midst of you**.

> Deuteronomy 7:15 And **the LORD will take away from you all sickness**...

God's heart is that there be no sickness amongst us whatsoever. He says that He will take away from us "all sickness". "All" means all!

100

Now, when it comes to praying for the sick, I would like to make a suggestion. Many times, when Christians pray for a sick person, they pray from a distance. For example, they might be at home and receive a call notifying them that someone is sick, and after the call they might pray for them right where they are. Now, in the earthly ministry of Jesus, thousands upon thousands of people were healed. For example, in Matthew 12:15, we read that the "multitudes" followed Jesus, and that "He healed them all". Now, out of all those thousands of people that He healed, how many did He heal from a distance? Well, in the Gospels, we are only told of **two** people who were healed from a distance. They were the centurion's servant and the Canaanite woman's daughter (Matthew 8:5-13; 15:22-28). These two cases clearly show us that healing definitely can happen when we pray from a distance. However, they also show us that such cases are the exception, and not the norm. Therefore, if we are to follow Jesus' example, we should normally actually go to the person who is sick. Jesus said about us:

> Mark 16:18 ... they will lay hands on the sick, and they will recover.

Notice that Jesus said that we would "lay hands on the sick". To lay hands requires that we are in close proximity to the sick person. In the book of Acts, we also see that all the healing miracles, except one, took place when the servant of God was near to the sick person. Even when God healed people through Peter's shadow, Peter was still in close

101

proximity to the sick persons. The only time we read of healing from a distance was when aprons and handkerchiefs from Paul were taken to the sick people. But even then, there was a physical object carrying the healing anointing. Furthermore, that particular instance is described as "unusual miracles" (Acts 19:11). The word "unusual" clearly indicates that this was not the norm. Lest I be misunderstood, I am not saying that God does not heal from a distance. Indeed, God can and does heal from a distance. We can't put God in a box! My point, however, is that the normal practice in the New Testament is that we go to the sick person. That's why James said that the sick person should "call for the elders of the church" and the elders were to "pray over him..." (James 5:14). This all describes close-range prayer. I have personally observed in my own experience that far more people are healed when I minister to them in person, then when I pray for them from a distance. Therefore, I encourage you to do what Jesus said – lay hands on the sick, and they will recover! When Jesus said they would lay hands on the sick, He was talking about **you**!

Now, if you are reading this, and you are sick in body, I am not saying that your healing is dependent on someone coming and laying hands on you. Indeed, you can lay hands on yourself and command that sickness to leave you in Jesus' name! I remember teaching on healing at a particular church. A few weeks later, I heard a testimony from a young lady who was present. As she was walking to work, she began to experience pain in her back. However, she remembered what I had taught about how we can command sickness to go. She commanded the pain to leave, and the pain left her straight away. Praise the Lord; nothing is impossible to those who believe! (Matthew 17:20).

Reflective Question:

1. Think about the way that you pray for other Christians? How might you modify this in light of what you have read in this chapter?

Chapter 11

What to Pray For – Part 4

Pray For Yourself

When teaching on prayer, Jesus taught that we should pray to God for ourselves. In His model prayer, He said:

> Matthew 6:11 Give us this day our daily bread.
> Matthew 6:12   And forgive us our debts, As we forgive our debtors.
> Matthew 6:13 And do not lead us into temptation, But deliver us from the evil one....

Jesus said, "Give us this day our daily bread". It is wonderful to know that we have a Father in heaven who will provide us with everything we need. Therefore, the apostle Paul was able to say:

> Philippians 4:6   Be anxious for nothing, but in everything by prayer and supplication, with thanksgiving, let your requests be made known to God;
> Philippians 4:7   and the peace of God, which surpasses all understanding, will guard your hearts and minds through Christ Jesus.

Here, the apostle exhorts us not to be anxious. Instead of tolerating anxiety, we are to let our requests be made known to God, but we are to do so "with thanksgiving". We are to thank God for the various things he has done for us. This will cause us to remember God's faithfulness to us. Such memories, coupled with the transference of our burdens to our Father, will cause us to experience "the peace of God" which will protect our hearts and minds, giving us the confidence that God has the matter covered. This peace "surpasses all understanding". Therefore, we do not need to know exactly how God will manifest the answer to our prayer, but we are at perfect peace because we know that He will.

Jesus also said, "And forgive us our debts, As we forgive our debtors". From time to time, we may slip up and sin. Therefore, John the apostle wrote the following:

> 1 John 2:1 My little children, these things I write to you, so that you may not sin. And if anyone sins, we have an Advocate with the Father, Jesus Christ the righteous.

John first says that the purpose of his writing is that we would not sin. This indicates that we are not to tolerate sin in our life. Because we love God, we do not want to sin against Him. Because of our sins, Jesus went through a horrible ordeal on the cross. Therefore, we should not want to continue to live in sin. However, if we do sin, John informs us that we have "an Advocate with the Father, Jesus

106

Christ the righteous". The word "Advocate" means that when we sin, Jesus Christ actually pleads our cause with the Father! In other words, He is our legal representative in heaven. Oh how Jesus loves us! But we should not think that the Father is mean whilst the Son is loving. No, it was the Father who sent the Son. It was because the Father loved us that He sent Jesus, so that we could have an "Advocate" to plead our cause to Him. That's why Jesus said:

John 3:16 For God so loved the world that He gave His only begotten Son, that whoever believes in Him should not perish but have everlasting life.
John 3:17 For God did not send His Son into the world to condemn the world, but that the world through Him might be saved.

It was the love of our Father that has sent Jesus to be our Advocate if we sin. Now, the Greek word translated "Advocate" is *parakletos* which also means a "comforter", "counsellor" and "helper". Isn't it wonderful to know that if we sin, Jesus is actually right there to offer us comfort? He is also there to help us overcome and to give His counsel. Oh what a loving Saviour we have! Let us not live under guilt and condemnation any more! Jesus is there to comfort us, to help us, and to counsel us if we sin. He is not there to condemn us. Condemnation comes from one source – the devil, who is also called the accuser of the brethren (Revelation 12:10). Therefore, the following passage

107

indicates that we are not to listen to the voices of accusation and condemnation:

> Romans 8:33 Who shall bring a charge against God's elect? It is God who justifies.
> Romans 8:34 Who is he who condemns? It is Christ who died, and furthermore is also risen, who is even at the right hand of God, who also makes intercession for us.

There are two reasons why we should not listen to the voices of accusation and condemnation. The first reason is because "it is God who justifies". The Greek word translated "justifies" means to "declare righteous". If we sin, we can confess our sins to God, and He immediately declares us righteous. That's why John also wrote:

> 1 John 1:9 If we confess our sins, He is faithful and just to forgive us *our* sins and to cleanse us from all unrighteousness.

Notice that the passage does not say, "if we confess our sins, He is faithful and just to give us a beating"! No, He is faithful and just to forgive us and to cleanse us from all unrighteousness. It is wonderful to know that when we confess our sins to God, He immediately forgives us. Hallelujah!

The second reason is because Christ, who is at the right hand of God, is making intercession for us as our Advocate.

108

He is in heaven as our legal representative, as our defence attorney. But why is it necessary for us to have a defence attorney? It is because there is also a prosecutor that is against us. John the apostle wrote the following:

> Revelation 12:9 So the great dragon was cast out, that serpent of old, called the Devil and Satan, who deceives the whole world; he was cast to the earth, and his angels were cast out with him.
> Revelation 12:10 Then I heard a loud voice saying in heaven, "Now salvation, and strength, and the kingdom of our God, and the power of His Christ have come, for the accuser of our brethren, who accused them before our God day and night, has been cast down.

These verses make it clear that we have an accuser – the devil. Unfortunately, in the above translation (NKJV), the phrase "who accused them before our God" is not accurately translated. The NKJV could leave you with the impression that the accusations of the devil only occurred in the past. However, in the original Greek, the word "accused" is in the *participle present* and should therefore be translated "is accusing". For this reason, Young's Literal Translation renders this verse more accurately as follows:

> Revelation 12:10 And I heard a great voice saying in the heaven, `Now did come the salvation, and the power, and the reign, of our God, and the authority of His Christ, because cast down was the accuser of

109

our brethren, who **is accusing** them before our God day and night;
(Young's Literal Translation)

The devil is presently accusing us before God day and night. But Jesus Christ is our defence lawyer! Furthermore, every time the devil accuses us he loses, because he has no answer for the blood of Jesus! Therefore, in the very next verse, John writes:

Revelation 12:11 And they overcame him [the devil] **by the blood of the Lamb** and by the word of their testimony, and they did not love their lives to the death.

We overcome the devil's accusations by the blood of Jesus Christ. This is because the blood of Jesus was shed so that our sins could be forgiven (Matthew 26:28). Therefore, whenever we need forgiveness, the answer is in the blood of Jesus. This means that the devil has no grounds on which to accuse us. God is perfectly just in forgiving our sins because Jesus paid the penalty for all our sins when He shed His blood. Therefore, Paul wrote:

Romans 3:25 ...God set forth [Jesus] as a propitiation by His blood...
Romans 3:26 ... that He [God] might be just and the justifier of the one who has faith in Jesus.

In these verses, Paul tells us that Jesus was set forth by God as a "propitiation by His blood". The word "propitiation" speaks of something that appeases one's wrath. Therefore, Paul is telling us that the shed blood of Jesus has appeased and fully satisfied God's wrath at sin and sinners. The outworking of this is that God is therefore perfectly just in justifying (declaring righteous) those who have faith in Jesus. Because we have put our faith in Jesus, we have been declared righteous, and God is perfectly just in doing that. Jesus, through His shed blood, has paid in full the penalty for our sins.

Knowing the power of the blood of Jesus ought to give us tremendous boldness and confidence when it comes to prayer. We can approach God knowing that there is nothing standing in between us and Him, because the blood of Jesus has taken care of it. We are completely righteous in His sight because of the blood of Jesus. Therefore, Paul wrote:

> 2 Corinthians 5:21 For He [God] made Him [Jesus] who knew no sin *to be* sin for us, that we might become the righteousness of God in Him.

Here Paul tells us that on the cross, Jesus was made sin. All our sins were transferred to Jesus on the cross and He paid the penalty for us. But that's not all. As a result of what Jesus did, we have been made "the righteousness of God in Him". In other words, now that we are in Christ, the righteous standard that God requires of man has been freely credited to us. We are completely righteous in God's sight!

It is important that when we approach God in prayer, we approach Him knowing that we are righteous in His sight. It will give us boldness in our prayers. This boldness is described in the following verse:

> Hebrews 10:19   Therefore, brethren, having boldness to enter the Holiest by the blood of Jesus...

We have boldness to enter God's presence. But this boldness is not because of our own goodness. No, it is based solely on the blood of Jesus Christ.

Now, when Jesus taught us to ask the Father for forgiveness, He made it plain that we are also to forgive others. This is very important, and we will pick up on this later on in this book.

Next, Jesus taught his disciples to pray that God would not lead them into temptation, but that He would deliver them from the evil one:

> Matthew 6:13 And do not lead us into temptation, But deliver us from the evil one....

Jesus said this before He went to the cross and purchased our redemption. Now that Jesus has died and risen again, all who believe in Him have already been delivered from the evil one. Therefore, Paul the apostle wrote the following:

> Colossians 1:13 [God] has delivered us from the power of darkness and conveyed us into the kingdom of the Son of His love,
> Colossians 1:14 in whom we have redemption through His blood, the forgiveness of sins.

Notice that the Father "**has** delivered us from the power of darkness". We don't need to be delivered from Satan anymore, because God has already delivered us from him. In the original Greek, the phrase "has delivered" is in the *aorist tense*, which denotes a completed action that has occurred in the past. Therefore, we no longer need to keep on praying that God would deliver us from the evil one – the devil is under our feet! However, he does still seek to destroy Christians. Regarding this, the apostle Peter wrote the following:

> 1 Peter 5:8 Be sober, be vigilant; because your adversary the devil walks about like a roaring lion, seeking whom he may devour.
> 1 Peter 5:9 Resist him, steadfast in the faith, knowing that the same sufferings are experienced by your brotherhood in the world.

Peter wrote this epistle to Christians who were suffering persecution (1 Peter 2:19-23; 3:14-17). In the above verses, Peter reveals that the devil was behind these persecutions. The devil's objective was to devour the Christians. However, Peter told these believers that they had the power to "resist" the devil. The Greek word translated "resist" is *anthistēmi* from which we get our English word "antihistamine". Now, if you suffer from hay fever, when the pollen count is high you may find that your nose begins to run and that you start sneezing etc. One thing you can do is to take an antihistamine tablet. The tablet won't remove the pollen, but it will remove the symptoms you are experiencing, rendering the negative effect of the pollen null and void. Even so, when we resist the devil, his attacks will not have his desired result. His weapons will not be able to prosper against us. That's why Paul was able to write the following:

> Ephesians 6:16 above all, taking the shield of faith with which you will be able to quench all the fiery darts of the wicked one.

When we take the shield of faith, and use it to resist the enemy, his fiery darts are quenched (i.e. extinguished!). They will not succeed in causing us harm. Furthermore, as we resist the devil, ultimately, he will have to flee from us. James said:

> James 4:7 Therefore submit to God. Resist the devil and he will flee from you.

The word "flee" suggests that he runs away utterly defeated. You will only "flee" from someone if you are afraid of him or her. When you resist the devil, he is afraid of you and runs away in a state of panic. He came like a roaring lion but runs off like the defeated foe that he is. We have authority over all the power of the enemy (Luke 10:19).

Before Jesus died on the cross for our redemption, we had not yet been delivered from the power of the enemy. Therefore, mankind had to pray "lead us into temptation, but deliver us from the evil one" (Matthew 6:13). Now that we have been delivered from the power of darkness, we have the authority and power to resist the devil's attacks and temptations, and he has to flee from us when we do so. We overcome the devil's temptations by walking in the Spirit. Paul said:

> Gal 5:16 I say then: Walk in the Spirit, and you shall not fulfill the lust of the flesh.

Through the Spirit, we can overcome the devil's temptations and walk free from the power of the flesh (i.e. sinful nature). However, the key to doing this is to set our minds on the things of the Spirit. About this, Paul wrote the following:

> Romans 8:5 For those who live according to the flesh set their minds on the things of the flesh, but those who live according to the Spirit, the things of the Spirit.

Notice that according to this verse, what we set our mind on determines what we do. If we mind fleshly things, then we will live according to the flesh. But if we mind the things of the Spirit, then we will live according to the Spirit, and will not fulfil the lust of the flesh.

Furthermore, an important key to overcoming temptation is to see ourselves the way that God sees us. Unfortunately, the reason that many Christians do not live victoriously is because they have not understood their new identity in relation to their old one. Many people fail to grasp what happened when they got born again. They think that they have just made a decision to turn from their old ways and to now serve Christ. But so much more has happened. Paul tells us of a very important and radical event that transpired when Jesus died:

> Romans 6:6   knowing this, that our old man was crucified with Him, that the body of sin might be done away with, that we should no longer be slaves of sin.

When Jesus died, the person we once were died with Him. The "you" that used to live in sin no longer exists; he has been crucified with Christ. We are now a totally "new creation" (2 Corinthians 5:17). But in order for this truth to become effective in our life, we need to see ourselves that way. That's why Paul went on to say:

> Romans 6:11   ... **reckon** yourselves to be dead indeed to sin, but alive to God in Christ Jesus our Lord.

A key word in this verse is "reckon", which in this context refers to the way we look at ourselves and perceive ourselves to be. We are to look at ourselves through the lens of God's word, which states that our old self died with

116

Jesus. We are therefore to see ourselves as truly being dead to sin, and alive to God. When we see ourselves in that way, we will not respond to sinful temptations because we are dead to sin. Even as a dead body doesn't respond if we speak to it, so we won't respond to temptation – we are dead to it. However, because we are alive to God, we will respond to what He wants us to do.

Pray For Your Enemies

Jesus also taught that we are to pray for our enemies:

> Luke 6:28 bless those who curse you, and pray for those who spitefully use you.

We are not to pray for their destruction, we are to pray God's blessing on them.

Two examples of praying this way for our enemies are the prayers of the Lord Jesus and Stephen at their death. When Jesus was being crucified, He prayed as follows:

> Luke 23:34 ..."Father, forgive them, for they do not know what they do."

Jesus even loved those who had crucified him, insomuch that He asked God to forgive them. When Stephen was being stoned to death, he said:

> Acts 7:60 ... "Lord, do not charge them with this sin."

Stephen realised that it was only by God's grace that he was saved. He therefore wanted that same grace to be extended to those who were stoning him. We must have the same heart towards those who mistreat us. We must love them and pray for them.

Reflective Questions:

1. Think about something you may have done recently that you know was not pleasing to God. How does knowing that Jesus is there for you as your Comforter if you sin, influence the way you relate to God?

2. Is there anyone in your life who has wronged you? How might you pray for them?

Chapter 12

Hindrances to Effective Prayer

In this chapter, we will look at eight things that can hinder our prayers in the New Covenant. If we want our prayers to be answered, it is essential that we avoid the following things.

1. Unbelief

It is essential that when we pray, we do so in faith. If we have unbelief, then we should not expect to receive the answer to our prayer. James said the following about doubting when we pray:

> James 1:6 But let him ask in faith, with no doubting, for he who doubts is like a wave of the sea driven and tossed by the wind.
> James 1:7 For let not that man suppose that he will receive anything from the Lord;
> James 1:8 he is a double-minded man, unstable in all his ways.

What James states here is very serious. He describes the person who doubts as unstable, and adds that such should not expect to receive anything from the Lord. In fact, elsewhere, the Bible reveals that faith is essential if we are to relate to God at all:

> Hebrews 11:6 But without faith *it is* impossible to please *Him,* for he who comes to God must believe that He is, and *that* He is a rewarder of those who diligently seek Him.

Without faith, we cannot please God. When we come to God, we must believe that He exists, and that He will respond positively to our request. This is what it means to believe that He is a rewarder to those who diligently seek Him. If we do not believe that God will respond positively to our request, then we are wasting our time by praying to Him. Remember, Jesus said:

> Matthew 21:22 And whatever things you ask in prayer, **believing**, you will receive.

When we pray, we must be actively "believing" if we wish to receive what we pray for. In other words, we must believe that what we are saying in prayer, is happening right there and then. As we speak our words of prayer, we must believe that they are happening as we speak them. Jesus said:

> Mark 11:23 Truly I say to you that whoever would say to this mountain, 'You must immediately be removed and you must immediately be cast into the sea,' and would not doubt in his heart but would

believe that what he is saying is happening, it will be to him.

(The One New Man Bible)

The above translation is a literal rendering of Mark 11:23. Notice that the person who speaks in faith, believes that what he is saying "is happening". He doesn't believe that it will one day happen. He doesn't wait for the answer before he believes it's happened. He believes that it is happening when he says it.

2. Half-hearted prayers

We saw in Chapter 3 that it is important to pray with our whole heart. Half-hearted prayer can be a hindrance to effective prayer. God doesn't want mere lip service, He wants our whole heart to be involved in prayer. Also, prayer can be quite an intense activity at times, and it is important that we pray through. In the following verse, Paul described the intensity with which Epaphras prayed:

> Colossians 4:12 Epaphras, who is *one* of you, a bondservant of Christ, greets you, always laboring fervently for you in prayers, that you may stand perfect and complete in all the will of God.

Epaphras is described as "laboring fervently" in prayer for the Colossians. The Greek word translated "laboring fervently" is *agōnizomai* from which we get the English word

121

"agonise". This suggests that his prayers were by no means casual. In fact, in the Greek translation of the Hebrew Old Testament (i.e. the Septuagint), *agonizomai* is used in Daniel 6:14 to describe the effort King Darius went to in order to free Daniel:

> Daniel 6:14 Then the king, when he heard the saying, was much grieved for Daniel and he greatly exerted [*agonizomai*] himself for Daniel to deliver him: and he exerted [*agonizomai*] himself till evening to deliver him.
> (Brenton)

The background to this passage is that King Darius had appointed Daniel as one of the three governors who were over the 120 satraps. However, Daniel distinguished himself above all of them because he had an excellent spirit, and the king was giving thought to setting Daniel over the whole kingdom. Now, the governors and the satraps knew that Daniel was a man of prayer, and so they plotted against him by convincing the king to sign a decree that anyone who petitioned any god for thirty days, except for the king, should be cast into the den of lions. However, Daniel did not compromise, and continued to pray faithfully. When the governors and satraps saw Daniel praying, they reported him to the king. However, the king did not want to throw Daniel into the lions' den. Nevertheless, according to the law of Medes and Persians, once signed, such a decree could not be changed. It so happened that the king was not able to find a way to deliver Daniel (although God did that

Himself by sending His angel to shut the lions' mouths!) Daniel 6:14, quoted above, describes how the king "greatly exerted" himself to find a way to rescue Daniel. In other words, he left no stone unturned in his quest to free Daniel. The Septuagint uses the word *agonizomai* to describe King Darius' effort, and this is the same word used of Epaphras' prayers in Colossians 4:12. Epaphras' prayers left no stone unturned, so that the Colossians would "stand perfect and complete in all the will of God". Like Ephapras, we need to labour with our whole heart in our prayers for others, believing that what we are praying is happening. As the Scriptures states:

> Psalm 119:145 I cry out with *my* **whole heart**; Hear me, O LORD! ...

3. Self-righteousness and pride

In the following parable, Jesus shows us the danger or self-righteousness and pride in relation to prayer:

> Luke 18:9 Also He spoke this parable to some who trusted in themselves that they were righteous, and despised others:
>
> Luke 18:10 "Two men went up to the temple to pray, one a Pharisee and the other a tax collector.
>
> Luke 18:11 The Pharisee stood and prayed thus with himself, 'God, I thank You that I am not like other

men—extortioners, unjust, adulterers, or even as this
tax collector.

Luke 18:12 I fast twice a week; I give tithes of all that I
possess.'

Luke 18:13 And the tax collector, standing afar off,
would not so much as raise *his* eyes to heaven, but
beat his breast, saying, 'God, be merciful to me a
sinner!'

Luke 18:14 I tell you, this man went down to his house
justified *rather* than the other; for everyone who
exalts himself will be humbled, and he who humbles
himself will be exalted."

The Pharisee's self-righteousness and pride was evident
from the fact that he looked down on the tax collector, and
also boasted of his own goodness – "I fast twice a week; I
give tithes of all that I possess" (Luke 18:12). The reason
that he looked down on the tax collector was because they
were known to collect more money than they should and
pocketed the excess. Therefore, tax collectors were
certainly not considered to be righteous. However, the
Pharisee was so caught up in his own self-righteousness
that he lost sight of his own shortcomings. We should stop
focusing on the faults of others and instead examine
ourselves.

Unlike the Pharisee, the tax collector knew that he was a
sinner, and because he confessed that to God, he went
away justified. Now, the tax collector doesn't represent the
born-again believer. As born-again believers, we certainly

shouldn't be coming to God "standing afar off", and not even raising our eyes to heaven. No, we are to approach God with boldness by the blood of Jesus (Hebrews 10:19). The tax collector represents someone who is not yet born-again but now realized that they are a sinner and so comes to God. However, this parable shows that God resists the proud, and so we must not approach God with any self-righteousness or pride.

4. Wrong motives

One reason why we may not receive what we are praying for is because we ask with the wrong motive. Regarding this, James wrote:

> James 4:3 You ask and do not receive, because you ask amiss, that you may spend *it* on your pleasures.

The persons that James describes in the above verse asked for the wrong reason – to satisfy their sinful pleasures. We should not expect to receive what we ask for when we ask with such motives.

Another wrong motive in prayer is the desire to impress others. About this, Jesus said the following:

> Matthew 6:5 "And when you pray, you shall not be like the hypocrites. For they love to pray standing

in the synagogues and on the corners of the streets, that they may be seen by men. Assuredly, I say to you, they have their reward.
Matthew 6:6 But you, when you pray, go into your room, and when you have shut your door, pray to your Father who *is* in the secret *place;* and your Father who sees in secret will reward you openly.

In this passage, Jesus describes certain "hypocrites" who prayed in public so that "they would be seen by men". Jesus is not saying that it is wrong to pray in public. For example, in a public gathering, you may be called upon to pray. There is nothing wrong with that. However, if your motive in doing so is to impress others, then that is wrong. The only reward you are promised for that kind of prayer is that men may well notice you. However, God is under no obligation to answer that kind of prayer. True prayer seeks the attention of God, not man.

5. Not honoring your wife

Peter wrote the following to Christian husbands:

1 Peter 3:7 Husbands, likewise, dwell with *them* with understanding, giving honor to the wife, as to the weaker vessel, and as *being* heirs together of the grace of life, that your prayers may not be hindered.

In this verse, Peter informs us that if a husband fails to give honour to his wife, it can negatively impact his prayers. The husband is to honour the wife in two ways. Firstly, he is to honour her as the "weaker vessel". Typically, a man will have superior physical strength to a woman. As the wife is physically weaker, the husband is to use his physical strength to do things for her that she may not be able to do. In other words, he is to use his physical strength to serve her. Secondly, he is to honour her as his equal partner in "the grace of life". The husband and wife are "heirs together" of this "grace", which speaks of equality. Whilst the husband is the head in the marital relationship, and the wife is to submit to him (typifying the relationship between Christ and the church, Ephesians 5:22-33) the husband and wife are nevertheless both **equal**. They just have different roles. The husband should love and treat his wife as his equal.

6. Unforgiveness and anger

The Bible reveals that both unforgiveness and anger can be a hindrance to effective prayer. Regarding unforgiveness, Jesus said:

> Mark 11:25 "And whenever you stand praying, if you have anything against anyone, forgive him, that your Father in heaven may also forgive you your trespasses.

127

Mark 11:26 But if you do not forgive, neither will your Father in heaven forgive your trespasses."

Regarding having anger in our hearts, Paul wrote:

1 Timothy 2:8 I desire therefore that the men pray everywhere, lifting up holy hands, **without wrath** and doubting;

It is important that we get rid of any unforgiveness or anger that we have towards anyone. Jesus went so far as to say that if we do not forgive, God will not forgive us. That is a very serious statement, and should be sufficient motivation for us to forgive.

In Matthew 18:21-35, Jesus told the parable of a man who owed the equivalent of millions of dollars to his master. This man couldn't pay his master, and so the master cancelled the debt. This same man then went and found someone who owed him the equivalent of a few thousand dollars, and threw him in prison until he should pay the debt. When the master found out about this, he was not at all pleased. His reaction is described in the following passage:

Matthew 18:34 And his master was angry, and **delivered him to the torturers** until he should pay all that was due to him.

Matthew 18:35 **"So My heavenly Father also will do to you** if each of you, from his heart, does not forgive his brother his trespasses."

When we refuse to forgive others, when God has forgiven us, I believe that it makes God "angry". Jesus here states that even as this master delivered his servant to the torturers, God will do precisely the same thing to us if we do not forgive from our heart the brother who sins against us.

Notice that in this parable, the master reversed the forgiveness he initially showed to his servant. The servant was forgiven, but when he refused to forgive someone else, that forgiveness was withdrawn, and now he was delivered to the torturers until he should pay the debt. Notice that Jesus said that God will do the same thing to us if we do not forgive our brother. In other words, we too will be delivered to the torturers until we pay back the debt that we owe God for our sins. The problem is that the penalty for our sins is eternity in hell (Revelation 20:15). And that is where we will end up if we do not forgive.

7. Not walking in love

Another hindrance to effective prayer is failure to walk in love towards our fellow Christians. About this, John the apostle wrote:

> 1 John 3:22 And whatever we ask we receive from Him, because we keep His commandments and do those things that are pleasing in His sight.
>
> 1 John 3:23 And **this is His commandment**: that we should believe on the name of His Son Jesus Christ and **love one another**, as He gave us commandment.

In verse 22, John states that the reason we receive what we ask for in prayer, is because we keep God's commandments. John then states that God's commandment is that we believe in the name of Jesus and love one another. Therefore, when we do not walk in love, our prayers become less effective. The apostle Paul describes this love in the following passage:

> [4] Love is patient, love is kind. It does not envy, it does not boast, it is not proud. [5] It does not dishonor others, it is not self-seeking, it is not easily angered, it keeps no record of wrongs. [6] Love does not delight in evil but rejoices with the truth. [7] It always protects, always trusts, always hopes, always perseveres.
> (1 Corinthians 13:4-7 NIV)

Wow! What a description. That is how we are to be to others. I would encourage you to re-read those verses again and again. This is what should characterize us as Christians. Every believer can walk in this love because God, who is love, lives inside us by His Spirit. When we walk in the Spirit, we will walk in His love.

8. Walking in unrighteousness

James conveyed the importance of righteousness in relation to prayer when he wrote the following:

> James 5:16 ...The effective, fervent prayer of a **righteous** man avails much.

The effective, fervent prayer of a righteous man avails much. Whilst we are the righteousness of God in Christ by faith, I don't believe that James is here referring to the free gift of righteousness. In this letter, James emphasizes practical righteousness, stating that "faith without works is dead" (James 2:20). James also points out that Abraham's works made his faith perfect (James 2:22). Therefore, when he speaks of "a righteous man" in James 5:16, it seems more likely that his emphasis in on someone who lives righteously. The prayers of such a person are said to avail much. However, the opposite is also true. If we are willfully living a sinful lifestyle, then our prayers will be less effective. If we sin, we should repent and confess that sin to God, and God will forgive us. As John said:

> 1 John 1:9 If we confess our sins, He is faithful and just to forgive us *our* sins and to cleanse us from all unrighteousness.

Therefore, let us put sin aside and walk in righteousness, knowing that we have a Father in heaven who forgives us if we stumble.

Reflective Questions:

1. Look through these eight hindrances to effective prayer. Which, if any, are present in your life? What will you do about that?

2. Look at the description of love found in 1 Corinthians 13:4-7. How does your attitude and behaviour compare to this description?

Chapter 13

The Prayer of Command

In the Bible, there are many examples of prayers being offered to God, in which the supplicant asks God to do a particular thing. However, there is also another form of prayer in which one speaks forth an authoritative command.

Joshua is one person who gives us a demonstration of this kind of prayer.

> Joshua 10:12 Then Joshua spoke to the LORD in the day when the LORD delivered up the Amorites before the children of Israel, and he said in the sight of Israel: "Sun, stand still over Gibeon; And Moon, in the Valley of Aijalon."
> Joshua 10:13 So the sun stood still, And the moon stopped, Till the people had revenge Upon their enemies. Is this not written in the Book of Jasher? So the sun stood still in the midst of heaven, and did not hasten to go down for about a whole day.
> Joshua 10:14 And there has been no day like that, before it or after it, that the LORD heeded the voice of a man; for the LORD fought for Israel.

Verse 12 informs us that Joshua spoke to the Lord (i.e. he prayed). Yet, when he prays, he doesn't ask God to do anything. Instead, he speaks directly to the sun and moon, commanding them to stand still. Joshua had faith that when he spoke to the sun and moon, God would cause them to be still. He was making use of another form of prayer in which, instead of pleading with God, we speak directly to the matter at hand, commanding it do what we desire.

Jesus also practiced this form of prayer. When He was about to raise Lazarus from the dead, He said the following:

> John 11:41 … "Father, I thank You that You have heard Me.
> John 11:42 And I know that You always hear Me, but because of the people who are standing by I said this, that they may believe that You sent Me."
> John 11:43 Now when He had said these things, He cried with a loud voice, "Lazarus, come forth!"

In verses 41 and 42, Jesus is praying to the Father. Yet, Jesus does not actually ask the Father to do anything. He simply thanks the Father that He had heard Him and that He always hears Him. Then, in verse 43, instead of asking God to raise up Lazarus, Jesus speaks directly to Lazarus and says "come forth!". In other words, Jesus was using the prayer of command. In fact, when ministering to the sick, Jesus never asked God to heal the sick person. He simply spoke the appropriate command, and the person was healed. For example, when a paralytic was brought to Him, He simply said "I say to you, arise, take up your bed, and go to your house" (Mark 2:11). That's how Jesus ministered to the sick, and He taught His disciples to do the same.

For example, when the lame man was healed in Acts 3, it was through a prayer of command that Peter uttered:

> Acts 3:6 Then Peter said [to the lame man], "Silver and gold I do not have, but what I do have I give you: In the name of Jesus Christ of Nazareth, **rise up and walk**."
> Acts 3:7 And he took him by the right hand and lifted him up, and immediately his feet and ankle bones received strength.

Again, on another occasion when Paul was ministering, he uttered a prayer of command so that a cripple could be healed:

> Acts 14:8 And in Lystra a certain man without strength in his feet was sitting, a cripple from his mother's womb, who had never walked.
> Acts 14:9 This man heard Paul speaking. Paul, observing him intently and seeing that he had faith to be healed,
> Acts 14:10 said with a loud voice, "**Stand up straight on your feet!**" And he leaped and walked.

In both these examples, Peter and Paul did not ask God to do anything. They simply uttered a prayer of command. I have learned in my walk with God that there are certain things that He doesn't want me to ask Him to do. Instead He wants me use the authority He has given me to command those things according to what I desire. Remember, we saw in Chapter 5 that we have been given Jesus' authority. Therefore, we can do the same things that He did. That's why He taught us to pray the prayer of command in Mark 11:23:

> Mark 11:23 Truly I say to you that whoever would say to this mountain, 'You must immediately be removed and you must immediately be cast into the sea,' and would not doubt in his heart but would believe that what he is saying is happening, it will be to him.
> (The One New Man Bible)

Notice that Jesus taught us to speak to the "mountain". A mountain is a physical object. It is important that we realise that physical objects can hear us when we speak to them. The day before Jesus said this, He was hungry and went to a fig tree. However, He found no fruit on it. Jesus therefore cursed the fig tree, declaring to it that no fruit would grow on it again. According to Matthew 21:19, the fig tree withered away "immediately". Now, what was Jesus doing speaking to a tree? Well, He knew that the fig tree could hear Him. It is important to realise that things can hear us, whether they are body parts, sicknesses, diseases, or demons. And when we speak to them in the name of Jesus, we are using the authority of Jesus Christ Himself.

The other thing I would like to point out from Mark 11:23 is that when we utter the prayer of command, we must do so in faith. This same verse reveals that in order to speak in faith, we must believe that what we are saying "is happening" there and then. There must be no doubt in our heart. We are to *know that we know that we know*, that what we are saying is happening there and then. By God's grace, I have seen many sick people healed in my ministry. But when I command the sickness out of them, right there and then, I believe that what I am saying is happening. I don't believe it when I see the results, I believe it is happening the moment I speak it. Therefore, when I ask them to test their condition, I fully expect them to say, "the pain has gone!". That's how faith works; it believes it receives the moment it speaks. Of course, it is not only raw faith that brings such healings. It is the healing anointing at work also[1].

Now, when it comes to ministering the prayer of command to bring healing to another person, God wants that person to participate in their healing. For example, when Peter walked on water, Jesus did not pick him up and place him on the water. Jesus simply said, "Come":

> Matthew 14:29 So He [Jesus] said, "Come." And when Peter had come down out of the boat, he walked on the water to go to Jesus.

After Jesus said, "come", Peter participated in the supernatural by getting down out of the boat, and starting to walk on the water. When he did this, the supernatural kicked

---

[1] For more information about the anointing, please see Dr. Stuart Pattico's book *The Anointing* which is available from: WWW.STUARTPATTICO.COM

137

in, and Peter realized he could walk on the water. The same applies to healing. God wants people to participate in their healing. Therefore, we find examples in the Gospels where Jesus asks the sick person to do a particular thing in relation to their miracle. For example, on a certain occasion, there was a man present who had a withered hand. This is what Jesus said to him:

> Luke 6:10 ..."Stretch out your hand." And he did so, and his hand was restored as whole as the other.

When the man participated in his healing by stretching out his hand, the healing miracle was manifested. This is why, once I command a sickness or disease out of someone, I ask them to immediately test the condition. This enables them to participate in their healing.

Another important way that God wants people to participate in their healing is through having faith. It is not only the person who utters the prayer of command who needs to have faith, but the person who is being ministered must have faith also. When the woman who had the issue of blood was healed, Jesus said to her, "**your faith** has made you well." (Matthew 9:22). Again, when a blind man was healed, Jesus said to him: "**your faith** has made you well." (Mark 10:52). Jesus also said the same thing to the Samaritan who was healed in Luke 17:19. This makes it clear that faith on the part of the recipient is crucial for the manifestation of the supernatural. Unbelief, however, can serve as a hindrance. When Jesus went to his hometown, He was not able to do many mighty works. Only a few healings took place. The reason is given to us in the following verses:

> Mark 6:5   Now He could do no mighty work there, except that He laid His hands on a few sick people and healed them.
> Mark 6:6   And He marveled because of their unbelief. Then He went about the villages in a circuit, teaching.

Their unbelief restricted Jesus. Matthew's gospel is even clearer:

> Matthew 13:58   Now He did not do many mighty works there **because of their unbelief**.

God wants us to have faith. He wants us to believe that He is who He says He is, and that He will do what He has promised.

Reflective Question:

1. What role do you think speaking prayers of command can have in your own prayer life?

Chapter 14

Praying According to God's Will

In 1 John 5:14-15, John the apostle said the following about prayer:

> 1 John 5:14 Now this is the confidence that we have in Him, that if we ask anything according to His will, He hears us.
>
> 1 John 5:15 And if we know that He hears us, whatever we ask, we know that we have the petitions that we have asked of Him.

In these verses, John informs us that we can be certain of answered prayer when we pray according to God's will. Unfortunately, John's words have been misunderstood by many Christians. Many believe that this means we need to add "if it be Your will" to the end of our prayers. Adding such a statement to the end of our prayers suggests that we are ignorant of God's will. Also, when the supplicant does not receive the answer to their prayer, they then conclude that it was not God's will. However, John does not suggest that we should add the phrase "if it be Your will" to the end of our prayers. The only time such a phrase appears in the New Testament is in James 4:15, and that verse is not even talking about prayer. There is also the time when a leper said to Jesus "if You are willing, You can make me clean" (Matthew 8:2). When Jesus saw the man's ignorance concerning His willingness to heal, He immediately corrected him and said "I am willing; be cleansed" (Matthew 8:3). If the leper had known the heart and compassion of Christ, he would never have doubted whether or not He was willing to heal him.

The truth is, when it comes to prayer, we can know the will of God. In Chapter 8, we have already observed that God's will can be seen by looking at heaven. In this chapter, we will look at three simple attributes that define the will of God. When we know these attributes, we then understand what God's will is, and can pray accordingly, being certain that "we have the petitions that we have asked of Him" (1 John 5:15).

The three attributes of God's will are given to us in Romans 12:2, where Paul writes:

> Romans 12:2   And do not be conformed to this world, but be transformed by the renewing of your mind, that you may prove what *is* that **good** and **acceptable** and **perfect will of God**.

In this verse Paul informs us that God's will is "good", "acceptable" and "perfect". If what we are praying for is "good", "acceptable" and "perfect", then we are praying according to God's will.

For example, when we are praying for those in authority, so that we can live "a quiet and peaceable life in all godliness and reverence", we know that we are praying according to

142

God's will because Paul states that this is "good and acceptable":

> 1 Timothy 2:1 Therefore I exhort first of all that supplications, prayers, intercessions, and giving of thanks be made for all men,
> 1 Timothy 2:2 for kings and all who are in authority, that we may lead a quiet and peaceable life in all godliness and reverence.
> 1 Timothy 2:3 For **this is good and acceptable in the sight of God** our Savior

If you are the son or daughter of a widow who needs financial support, and you are praying for finances to be able to provide this, then you are praying according to God's will. Paul states that this is the case in 1 Timothy 5:3-4:

> 1 Timothy 5:4 But if any widow has children or grandchildren, let them first learn to show piety at home and to repay their parents; for **this is good and acceptable before God**.

If you are praying for a sick person to be healed, then you are praying according to God's will, because Acts 10:38 calls healing "good":

> Acts 10:38 how God anointed Jesus of Nazareth with the Holy Spirit and with power, who went about **doing good** and **healing all** who were oppressed by the devil, for God was with Him.

143

Jesus' healing is described as Him "doing good". God's will is "good" which means that healing is always consistent with His will. Jesus described His activities (including healing) as "good works" in John 10:32.

If what you are praying for is in accordance with righteousness, peace, and joy, then you are praying according to God's will. Paul the apostle wrote the following:

> Romans 14:17 for the kingdom of God is not eating and drinking, but righteousness and peace and joy in the Holy Spirit.
> Romans 14:18 For he who serves Christ in these things is **acceptable** to God...

If something lines up with righteousness, peace and joy, then it is part of the "acceptable" will of God, as Paul said that those who serve Christ that way are "acceptable to God".

We have seen a few examples of God's "good" and "acceptable" will. But Romans 12:2 also states that God's will is "perfect". God doesn't want you to have something that is just nice. He doesn't want you to have the second best. He doesn't want you to have something that you would rate 4 out of 5. He wants you to have that which is perfect! He wants you have the very best. James said:

144

James 1:17 Every good gift and **every perfect gift is from above**, and comes down from the Father of lights

What God gives is good and perfect. It is time to take the limits off God in our prayers. Let's believe that God can give us the very best when we pray.

Jesus didn't teach us to pray with limitations in our mind. Consider what He said to His disciples about prayer in the following passage:

John 15:7 If you abide in Me, and My words abide in you, you will ask what you desire, and it shall be done for you

If you abide in Christ, and His words abide in you, then you can ask "**what you desire**". That is a powerful promise. What about you? Are you abiding in Christ? Do His words abide in you? Well, what do you desire? Ask for it, and "it shall be done for you"!

Before we go onto the next chapter, I would like to point out something else that 1 John 5:14-15 reveals:

1 John 5:14 Now this is the confidence that we have in Him, that if we ask anything according to His will, He hears us.

> 1 John 5:15   And if **we know that He hears us**, whatever we ask, we know that we have the petitions that we have asked of Him.

Now, in the Old Testament, there are various examples of people asking God to hear their prayer. However, under the New Covenant, we don't need to ask God to hear our prayer. Notice that according to the above passage, when we pray according to God's will "we **know** that He hears us". The is the "confidence" that we have in Him. We don't need to plead with God to hear our prayers. When we pray, we "know" that He hears, and its important that we pray with that awareness. That's the way Jesus prayed. In John 11:41-42 He said:

> John 11:41 ... "Father, I thank You that **You have heard Me**.
> John 11:42   And I know that **You always hear Me**, but because of the people who are standing by I said this, that they may believe that You sent Me."

Jesus walked in the awareness that His Father always heard Him. As we are in Christ, we need to walk in that awareness too. When we do, we will not need to plead with God to hear our prayer, for we "know that He hears us".

Reflective Questions:

1. What things do you desire from God?

2. Would you consider those things to be "good", "acceptable" and "perfect"?

3. Are there good things that you desire, but haven't asked God for, because you don't think that He would be gracious enough to give them to you?

4. Are you willing to remove any limitations you have imposed on God, and to boldly ask for whatever you desire?

Chapter 15

Worshiping in Spirit and Truth – Part 1

One of the exciting things about prayer is that it gives us an opportunity to worship God. The first time the word "worship" appears in our English Bibles is in Genesis 22:5. God had told Abraham to offer his son Isaac as a burnt offering. Early the next morning, Abraham took Isaac, as well as two other men, and went to do what God had instructed him to do. At a certain point, Abraham said the following to the two men:

> Genesis 22:5 ..."Stay here with the donkey; the lad and I will go yonder and **worship**, and we will come back to you."

As far as Abraham was concerned, he and Isaac were going to "worship". The Hebrew word here translated "worship" is *shâchâh* which means to humbly beseech, to bow down, crouch or prostrate oneself. When you appear before human royalty, it is in order to respectfully bow down. How much more should we not "worship" when we come before God who is the great King? However, the narrative of Abraham proceeding to offer up Isaac reveals that true worship goes beyond the literal definition of the word. Jesus indicated this when He said:

John 4:24 God *is* Spirit, and those who worship Him must worship in spirit and truth.

We are to worship in spirit and in truth, and the purpose of the next two chapters is to help you to do just that.

It is interesting to note that for Abraham, offering up Isaac was an act of "worship". This story therefore informs us of several important elements that constitute true worship. We will look at them one by one.

Worship is an act of faith

In Genesis 21:12, God had informed Abraham that it was through Isaac that His promise to Abraham would be fulfilled. Therefore, how could God now require that Abraham sacrifice Isaac? Hebrews 11:17-19 gives us incredible insight as to what Abraham believed would happen:

Hebrews 11:17 By faith Abraham, when he was tested, offered up Isaac, and he who had received the promises offered up his only begotten son,
Hebrews 11:18 of whom it was said, "In Isaac you seed shall be called,"
Hebrews 11:19 concluding that God was able to raise him up, even from the dead, from which he also received him in a figurative sense.

Abraham believed that if he offered up Isaac, God would raise him up from the dead! That's how sure he was of God's promise. That's possibly why Abraham said to the two men "**we** [i.e. both he and Isaac] will come back to you" (Genesis 22:5). Therefore, Abraham's act of worship was an act of faith.

All true worship is to be done in faith. For starters, we are worshipping Someone we cannot see. Therefore, faith is required. We must believe that God is there. Hebrews 11:6 says the following about this:

> Hebrews 11:6 But without faith it is impossible to please Him, for he who comes to God must believe that He is, and that He is a rewarder of those who diligently seek Him.

According to this verse, we must believe that God is. However, it doesn't stop there. We must also believe that He is a "rewarder". In other words, we must believe that He receives and responds to our worship. As we worship God, we must be aware that He is receiving our offering and responding to it. Worship is an act of faith.

Worship is rooted in the fear of God

As Abraham was about to offer up Isaac, the angel of the Lord stopped him, and revealed something very important about what was behind Abraham's act of worship:

Genesis 22:12 And He [the angel of the Lord] said, "Do not lay your hand on the lad, or do anything to him; for **now I know that you fear God**, since you have not withheld your son, your only son, from Me."

Abraham's willingness to offer Isaac demonstrated that he feared God. All true worship must be rooted in the fear of the Lord. Now, in Chapter 4, we saw that God does not want us to be afraid of Him (Romans 8:15). He wants us to approach him without fear. So what do I mean by "the fear of the Lord"? Well, "the fear of the Lord" is not being afraid to approach God. It is something else entirely different, which is evident when we consider an important episode in Israel's history.

After the Israelites went out of Egypt. God came and visited them on Mount Sinai. Exodus 19:18 describes the scene as follows:

Exodus 19:18 Now Mount Sinai *was* completely in smoke, because the LORD descended upon it in fire. Its smoke ascended like the smoke of a furnace, and the whole mountain quaked greatly.

The mountain itself was shaking because of God's presence. God gave Israel a glimpse of His power and glory. When on the mountain, God began to speak in an audible voice to the Israelites, giving them what became known as the Ten Commandments. After God reached number ten, the

Israelites were very afraid, and thought they were going to die. So they asked Moses to speak to God and to receive the rest of the Law from God, and that Moses would speak the rest of the Law to them instead of God (Exodus 20:18-19). What Moses then said to them gives us great insight into what the fear of God is:

> Exodus 20:20 And Moses said to the people, "Do not fear; for God has come to test you, and that **His fear** may be before you, so that you may not sin."

Notice that Moses mentions two types of fear in this verse. He first says "Do not fear", but then he speaks of "His (God's) fear". Let's have a look at this:

The first thing that Moses said was "Do not fear". In other words, do not be afraid – God has not come to destroy you. It is so important to realize that the fear of the Lord is not about being afraid that God is about to strike you dead. That is not the true fear of the Lord. Also, the true fear of God is not when you are so afraid of God that you dare not even approach Him. It is essential that we realize that the fear of God is not about that. That is the wrong kind of fear. Indeed, our Lord Jesus shed His blood so that we can "draw near" to God and have a relationship with Him (John 3:16; 17:3).

Moses then said something very interesting. He said, "...God has come to test you, and that **His fear** may be before you, so that you may not sin". We must not have the wrong kind of fear. But we must have the correct kind of fear - "His (God's) fear". In other words, Moses was saying: "God hasn't come to kill you. He doesn't want you to be afraid that He is going to do that. But He has come so that you may see how awesome and powerful He is, so that you may always have a healthy fear of Him so that you won't dare sin against Him". The true fear of God is knowing how awesome and powerful God is, and consequently not daring to be so unwise as to sin against Him. No wonder Proverbs 9:10 says that "the fear of the LORD is the beginning of wisdom...". You probably wouldn't mess with someone armed with a machine gun, so why mess with God? We need to recapture a correct view of God. He is more powerful and awesome than we can imagine. No wonder the psalmist said:

Psalm 33:8 Let all the earth fear the LORD; Let all the inhabitants of the world stand in awe of Him.

Our awesome God is said in Isaiah 40:12, to have measured the entire universe with the span of His hand. Let us consider that our universe has billions of galaxies, each containing billions of stars. When we look at the sky at night, we only see a portion of the galaxy in which we live, called the Milky Way. Within our galaxy, the nearest star to the earth is the sun. If we were to fly to the sun by a commercial airplane, it would take about 21 years to get there. If we were to travel by that same airplane to the next nearest star in our galaxy, it would take over five million years... and that is within our galaxy. When we consider that there are billions of other galaxies, each having billions of stars, we begin to understand how huge our universe is. Yet God measured all of that with the span of His hand!

Our God is much bigger than the entire universe. That is what Solomon meant when He said:

> 1 Kings 8:27 "...Behold, heaven and the heaven of heavens cannot contain You..."

The first reference to "heaven" in this verse is not a reference to where God lives, but to the realm that we see in the night sky (i.e. outer space, the rest of the universe). The second reference to "the heaven of the heavens" refers the place where God lives. Therefore, Solomon is saying that outer space, and heaven where God lives cannot contain the presence of God. God is bigger than them both!

It is interesting that not even heaven itself witnesses the fullness of God's glory. Isaiah 66:1 calls heaven God's throne. A throne is something that is sat upon. However, in order for God to sit, He must lower Himself, which may indicate that even heaven does not witness the fullness of God's power. In order for God to communicate with the world, it seems that He must then lower Himself again. He does this by borrowing creaturely terms to describe Himself, such as "hand" and "eye" etc. so that He can communicate Himself to us. This self-lowering of God is possibly alluded to Psalm 18:10:

Psalm 18:10 And He rode upon a cherub, and flew; He flew upon the wings of the wind.

The verb "rode" may indicate that He leaves His natural state where He is absolutely unknowable and inconceivable (1 Timothy 6:16). He is then said to fly "upon the wings of the wind". The term "wings", which can allude to "coverings", may indicate that God covers and conceals His glory, not revealing it completely, lest His awesome glory blinds His creatures.

One who has an awareness of the vastness, awesomeness, might and power of God will automatically bow down before Him in awe, regarding and honouring Him above all else. This is what the fear of the Lord is.

Another passage in Exodus that conveys to us the nature of the fear of the Lord is found in Exodus 9:20-21. God had said that He was about to send hailstones. The response of the Egyptians was as follows:

Exodus 9:20 He who **feared** the word of the LORD among the servants of Pharaoh made his servants and his livestock flee to the houses.
Exodus 9:21 But he who did not **regard** the word of the LORD left his servants and his livestock in the field.

These two verses use the words 'feared' and 'regard' interchangeably. From this we can see that the fear of the

Lord involves highly regarding God above all, knowing the endlessness of His power. Abraham's act of worship was rooted in this state of heart. He did not take it upon himself to question the Almighty, but regarded God's Word above anything else, including his own wisdom. This is the fear of the Lord.

Reflective Questions:

1. What role does faith play in your personal times of worship?

2. How do you think walking in "the fear of the Lord" will impact your worship and everyday life?

Chapter 16

Worshiping in Spirit and Truth – Part 2

Worship is a sacrifice

It is interesting that when Abraham said they were going to "worship" (Genesis 22:5), he was in fact about to sacrifice his son Isaac. This shows us that true worship is a sacrifice that we offer to God.

In the New Covenant, we no longer bring animal sacrifices to God. However, the New Testament uses the term 'sacrifice' with reference to financial giving (Philippians 4:16-19; Hebrews 13:16) and with reference to "the sacrifice of praise" (Hebrews 13:15). It is beyond the scope of this book to look at financial giving (although that is part of worship) as we are dealing with prayer. However, we will look at the sacrifice of praise as that has particular relevance to prayer. As we saw in Chapter 1, one of the reasons that we pray is to give God praise (Isaiah 12:4). Regarding the sacrifice of praise, Hebrews 13:15 states:

> Hebrews 13:15 Therefore by Him let us continually offer the sacrifice of praise to God, that is, the fruit of *our* lips, giving thanks to His name.

By seeing praise as a "sacrifice", it becomes evident that there is a link between praise and worship. Worship is a sacrifice, and part of that sacrifice is to offer God praise. King David was used by God in this area. The Holy Spirit inspired David to write many of the psalms. The Hebrew word for Psalm is *tehillim*. This word comes from the Hebrew root *halal* which is normally translated as "praise". However, *halal* has two other meanings which are also very significant. *Halal* also carries the meaning of brightness and shining. An example of this use of *halal* is in Job 29:3:

> Job 29:3 When His lamp shone [*halal*] upon my head...

When we praise God, we shine. We beam with spiritual light (glory) as we give our praises to God.

Another connotation of the Hebrew word *halal* is that of "madness". This indicates that there are depths of worship that go beyond the realm of logic, and can result in expressions that may outwardly appear to be crazy or even mad!

The company of prophets were known for praising God. 1 Samuel 10:5 indicates that the prophets made use of various musical instruments when prophesying:

> 1 Samuel 10:5 ... you will meet a group of prophets coming down from the high place with a stringed instrument, a tambourine, a flute, and a harp before them; and they will be prophesying.

160

The use of these instruments indicates that praise is an important aspect of the prophetic. However, the prophets were also known as madmen. On one occasion, a certain prophet gave a word from the Lord to Jehu. After the prophet had left, Jehu's companions came to him and said:

> 2 Kings 9:11 "*Is* all well? Why did this **madman** come to you?"

Evidently, the prophets were known to enter into a zone of experience that went beyond what the observer could consider normal. These prophets were considered mad! We therefore need to be open to the fact that as we offer to God the sacrifice of praise, and offer up true *halal* we may well enter into realms of expression that may seem rather bizarre to the onlooker.

Psalm 22:3 tells us that God is enthroned in our praises. The throne is for the King. When we praise God, His kingly power is demonstrated in our lives. The devil knows this, and will therefore attempt to prevent us from praising God. We must be diligent to resist the devil's strategy, as it is his attempt to rob us of experiencing God's power. Isaiah the prophet wrote the following:

> Isaiah 54:1 ...Break forth into singing...

Sometimes, before we can truly enter into expressive praise, we need to "break forth". We need to break through the emotions associated with our negative circumstances. We may need to break through the forces of darkness that seek to keep us in a lukewarm zone of praise. The Hebrew word translated "break forth" (*patsach*) in Isaiah 54:1 is related to the Hebrew root *patzah* which means "to open", and to the root *patzatz* which means 'to explode". Interestingly, a key Greek word for the Holy Spirit's power is *dunamis*, from which we get our English word "dynamite". The dynamite of the Holy Spirit inside us enables us to experience an explosion (*patzatz*) of spiritual power in our soul, which causes us to "open" (*patzah*) our mouth in true *halal*. We have thus broken through everything that tried to prevent us from praising God, and are able to experience and express the unspeakable joy of His presence.

As we offer to God the sacrifice of praise, there are various physical expressions that may accompany it. Such expressions include:

Singing:

> Psalm 100:2 Serve the LORD with gladness; Come before His presence with singing.

Dancing:

> Psalm 149:3 Let them praise His name with the dance;

Clapping our hands

Psalm 47:1 Oh, clap your hands, all you peoples!

Shouting:

Psalm 5:11 Let them ever shout for joy...

Lifting our hands:

Psalm 63:4 Thus I will bless You while I live;
I will lift up my hands in Your name.

Musical expressions:

Psalm 33:2 Praise the LORD with the harp; Make
melody to Him with an instrument of ten strings.
Psalm 33:3 Sing to Him a new song; Play skillfully
with a shout of joy.

Psalm 150:5 Praise Him with loud cymbals; Praise
Him with clashing cymbals!

However, let's also remember that the Hebrew word for
worship (shâchâh) means to humbly beseech, to bow down,
crouch or prostrate oneself. There will be times when God's

presence is so strong that we simply have to be still, or bow before Him in total reverence.

Worship is ultimately offering ourselves to God

In Genesis 22:5, Abraham did not say to the two men that only he was going to worship. He explicitly stated that both he and Isaac were going to worship:

> Genesis 22:5 ..."Stay here with the donkey; **the lad and I** will go yonder and worship, and we will come back to you."

Therefore, in order to understand what true worship is, we need to appreciate the role that Isaac played in this. It is essential that we realize that Isaac was not a small child when he went with Abraham to be sacrificed. This is evident from Genesis 22:6 which reveals that Isaac was old enough to be able to carry a sufficient load of wood to make a fire that would consume a burnt offering:

> Genesis 22:6 So Abraham took the wood of the burnt offering and laid *it* on Isaac his son; and he took the fire in his hand, and a knife, and the two of them went together.

The Jewish historian Josephus, states that Isaac was 25 years old, and other ancient writers even suggest that he was in his thirties. Yet, we do not read that Isaac even attempted to resist his father when he proceeded to offer him up, even though he was old enough and strong enough to do so.

So, what was Isaac's part in this act of worship? Isaac's worship was that he was completely willing to lay down his life at his fathers command. And this is what true worship ultimately is. In addition to offering our praises to God, worship is about offering ourselves to God. Therefore, Paul the apostle wrote the following:

> Therefore, I urge you, brothers, in view of God's mercy, to offer your bodies as living sacrifices, holy and pleasing to God—this is your spiritual act of worship.
> (Romans 12:1, NIV)

Notice that Paul described "worship" as offering our bodies as living sacrifices to God. True worship will always lead us to a place where we are surrendering ourselves to God. As we surrender ourselves to God in prayer, we are truly worshipping God.

Jesus Himself did this, shortly before going to the cross. As He prayed to the Father, He asked God that if it were possible, that the forthcoming experience of enduring the cross be taken away from him. Here are His words:

Luke 22:42 "Father, if it is Your will, take this cup away from Me; nevertheless not My will, but Yours, be done."

In His humanity, Jesus did not want to endure the cross. Not because He didn't love us, but because He was about to bear the sins of the whole world. However, He knew that it was God's will that He endure it, and so in this prayer, He surrendered Himself to God's will. That He already knew that it was God's will is evident from Matthew 20:28 where He said that He had come to give His life a ransom for many. Luke 22:42 is the only time we find a prayer in the Bible where someone says "not My will, but Yours, be done" and the context is that Jesus is surrendering to what He knows the Father wanted Him to do. When we know that God wants us to do something, that in our humanity we may not wish to do, we too can pray that prayer: "not My will, but Yours, be done". In so doing, we are offering ourselves up to God, surrendering our will to His, and giving ourselves totally to Him. This is true worship.

Reflective Questions:

1. What experiences have you had of God when praising Him? What experiences would you like to have?

2. Are there areas of your life that you have not yet surrendered to God? What are they and what will you now do?

Summary

Here are some points that summarize what has been covered by this book:

- Prayer is calling upon God
- You can pray to draw near to God, praise God, give thanks, confess your sins, ask God a question, and to make requests of God
- You must pray in faith, which means that you believe that what you are saying is happening there and then
- You must pray with your whole heart
- You are to pray to the Father in the name of Jesus Christ
- The devil is a zero. Jesus has totally defeated him.
- We have been given the authority of Jesus Christ, and we can use that authority by using His name
- When you pray in tongues, your spirit prays, you access the hidden wisdom of God, you offer up perfect praise to God, you pray according to God's perfect will, and you build yourself up in God
- We are to pray for the purposes of God, for secular leaders, that God would send out workers, for existing preachers of the gospel, for all the saints, for ourselves, and for our enemies
- It is always God's will to heal
- Eight hindrances to effective prayer are: unbelief, half-hearted prayers, self-righteousness / pride, wrong motives, not honouring your wife,

unforgiveness / anger, not walking in love, and walking in unrighteousness
- You can utter prayers of command
- You can know the will of God and pray accordingly
- If what you are praying for is good, acceptable, and perfect, then you are praying according to God's will
- You don't need to plead with God to hear your prayers under the New Covenant, you can know that He hears you
- Four aspects of true worship are that it is an act of faith, it is rooted in the fear of God, it is a sacrifice, and it is ultimately offering yourself to God

Thank you for having taken the time to read this book. It is my prayer that the teachings in the book will help you in your prayer life. I would recommend that you use this book as a handbook that you can refer to again and again. You may also want to read it again now to ensure that you have laid hold of the various truths this book contains.

Shalom.

Appendix

The Correct Translation of Luke 23:43

Due to a mistranslation of Luke 23:43, many people have mistakenly thought that Jesus immediately went to Paradise when He died. However, we have seen from Chapter 5 that Jesus went to the Abyss in Hades when he died. Jesus didn't go to Paradise until His ascension. In the NKJV, Luke 23:43 reads as follows:

> Luke 23:43 And Jesus said to him [the thief on the cross], "Assuredly, I say to you, today you will be with Me in Paradise."

In the NKJV, the comma is placed after the phrase, "I say to you" so that "today" is connected to "you will be with Me in Paradise". However, in the Greek there is no punctuation, and so the translators must decide where they put the comma. The following two translations place the coma in a different place which gives a totally different reading;

> (Lamsa) Truly I say to you today, You will be with me in Paradise.

> (Tomanek) Indeed today I say to you, you shall be with Me in paradise.

171

The above two translations do not give the impression that Jesus would be in Paradise that same day. Rather, the phrase "I say to you today" is an idiom that denotes solemn expression. That Lamsa and Tomanek place the comma in the correct location is evident when we consider the following about the Greek language.

The Greek word for "today" is *sēmeron*. In Greek, when *sēmeron* comes after a verb, it belongs to that verb, unless it is separated from the verb by the Greek word *hoti*. When *hoti* separates *sēmeron* from the verb, then *sēmeron* belongs to the next clause. For example, Mark 14:30 is an example where *sēmeron* belongs to the next clause because *hoti* separates it from the verb.

> Mark 14:30 Jesus said to him, "Assuredly, I say [verb] to you that [*hoti*] today [*sēmeron*], *even* this night, before the rooster crows twice, you will deny Me three times."

In this verse "today" refers to what comes later, namely that Peter would deny Christ three times. On the other hand, Matthew 21:28 is an example where *sēmeron* belongs to the preceding verb because *hoti* is not present in the verse to separate it:

> Matthew 21:28 "But what do you think? A man had two sons, and he came to the first and said, 'Son, go, work [verb] today [*sēmeron*] in my vineyard.'

In this verse, "today" refers to the verb "work" which precedes it, so that the "work" is to be done "today". This is because *hoti* is not present in the verse to separate *sēmeron* from the verb "work".

In Luke 23:43, the Greek word *hoti* is not there, which means that *sēmeron* belongs the verb "I say" and not to the next clause - "you will be with Me in paradise":

> "Truly I say [verb] to you today [*sēmeron*], You will be with me in Paradise"

Therefore, the comma should come after "today", as per Lamsa and Tomanek, so that "today" belongs to the phrase, "I say to you" and not to "you will be with Me in Paradise". This use of language is quite similar to what we find in Deuteronomy 6:6 where Moses said:

> Deuteronomy 6:6   And these words, which I command thee this day, shall be in thine heart:
> (KJV)

In this verse, "this day" refers to the words that God commanded them, and not to "shall be in your heart", and therefore the comma is placed after "this day". The same should also have been done in Luke 23:43.

Booking Dr. Stuart & Andrea Pattico

Thank you for reading this book. To invite Dr. Stuart Pattico to speak at your church, conference, event, or ministry school, please contact him by going to the 'Contact Us' page on the below website. Dr. Pattico ministers on many subjects, and is available for national / international preaching and teaching engagements, healing meetings, seminars, leadership training etc. His wife, Minister Andrea Pattico, is also available to speak and lead worship at worship events. Here is their website, where both Dr. Stuart & Andrea Pattico can be contacted:

WWW.STUARTPATTICO.COM

The above website also has many free articles which you can read, and many videos and audio messages that you can freely watch / listen to. On this site, you can also join the free mailing list to receive regular ministry updates, and notifications when new resources are added to this site.

SUNESIS BIBLE COLLEGE

Equipping the Saints

Sunesis Bible College is a Spirit-filled, distance learning Bible school, founded by Rev. Dr. Stuart Pattico. Whether your wish to study for ministry, or for your own personal development, we have exciting courses for you!

All lectures are sent to your home on CD, along with all the required reading material and the course guide. You are also given access to a personal tutor. Our courses include:

- Mastering the Bible
- Knowing Who You Are in Christ
- How to be Led by the Holy Spirit and Hear God's Voice
- The Authority of the Believer
- Prayer – Bringing Heaven to Earth
- Praise and Worship
- Understanding the Anointing
- The Gifts of the Spirit
- How to Receive and Minister God's Healing Power
- Fivefold Ministry
- Miracle Evangelism
- Church Administration
- God's Plan for Israel

For more information, please visit:

WWW.SUNESISBIBLECOLLEGE.COM

Other Resources by Dr. Stuart Pattico

Books:

End Times   *The Anointing*   *Understanding the Bible*
(Study Guide)

Booklets:

Interpret Your Dreams   *You Can Prophesy*

These resources, as well as CDs of Dr. Pattico's messages are available from:

WWW.STUARTPATTICO.COM

Join Our Mailing List

Our website, WWW.STUARTPATTICO.COM contains free videos that you can watch, articles that you can read, and many audio messages that you can freely listen to. On this site, you can also join the free mailing list by submitting your email address. You will then receive regular ministry updates, and notifications when new items are added to this site.

Become a Ministry Partner

In obedience to God's call, Dr. Stuart Pattico left his secular employment to devote himself to his preaching and teaching ministry on a full-time basis. If you would like to financially support Dr. Pattico's full-time ministry, you can do so by either making a one-off donation, or by making automatic monthly payments by setting up a standing order. Please visit the donation section of our website for more information:

WWW.STUARTPATTICO.COM

Publish Your Book With Us!

Sunesis Publications helps Christian authors to publish their God-given books.

With our low-cost, professional publishing package, you keep all the profit from your book sales **(not only a royalty payment)! As your publisher, here is what we do:**

- We send you **50* printed copies** of your book as part of the package.
- We allocate an ISBN to your book.
- We design a cover for your book
- We place a barcode on your book
- We get your manuscript into a print-ready format
- We take care of the legalities of sending copies of your book to the British Library (a legal requirement in the UK) and other deposit libraries.

Once your book is published, we can then print "on demand" more copies of your book as and when you need them (we print a minimum of 50 copies). This means that you will not need to worry about storing a large volume of books, as we simply print what you need.

For more information, please visit:
WWW.STUARTPATTICO.COM

We reserve the right not to publish any book for any reason. We will only publish Christian books that are in agreement with the values of Sunesis Publications, and do not promise to publish every Christian book submitted to us. We will not publish any book that we do not feel led of the Lord to publish.

---

* *The number of books may vary. The number of books you receive depends on the size of your book, the number of pages, and whether or not your book's interior includes any colour etc.*